*International
Monetary Issues
after the Cold War*

INTERNATIONAL MONETARY ISSUES AFTER THE COLD WAR

A Conversation among Leading Economists

Edited by Randall Hinshaw

The Johns Hopkins University Press
Baltimore and London

The Johns Hopkins University Press
2715 North Charles Street
Baltimore, Maryland 21218-4319
The Johns Hopkins Press Ltd., London

Library of Congress
Cataloging-in-Publication Data

International monetary issues after the cold war : a
    conversation among leading economists / edited by
    Randall Hinshaw.
        p.   cm.
    Includes indexes.
    ISBN 0-8018-4538-6 (alk. paper)
        1. International finance—Congresses.
    2. Monetary policy—Congresses.   I. Hinshaw,
    Randall Weston.
    HG207.I557   1993
    332'.042—dc20   92-26323

A catalog record for this book is
available from the British Library.

To the Memory of

The Honorable Willard L. Thorp

1899–1992

Founding Chairman of the

Bologna-Claremont Dialogues

Contents

Contributors ix

Foreword xi
  John David Maguire

Prologue 1
  Randall Hinshaw

1. Exploration of the Issues 5
  Introduced by Robert A. Mundell

2. U.S. Issues: Ten Views 13
  Introduced by Milton Friedman

3. U.S. Monetary and Fiscal Dilemmas and Options 23
  Introduced by Paul A. Samuelson

4. Monetary Problems of German Unification 37
  Introduced by Otmar Issing

5. International Policy Coordination Reconsidered 61
  Introduced by Jeffrey A. Frankel

6. Monetary Issues in Western Europe 75
  Introduced by Christopher Johnson

7. The Issue of Regionalism 114
  Introduced by Robert A. Mundell

8. Monetary Issues in Eastern Europe 124
  Introduced by Richard N. Cooper

9. Economic Science Grapples with Dilemmas
  of International Finance 149
  Paul A. Samuelson

Name Index 157

Subject Index 159

Contributors

Sven W. Arndt, Professor of Economics, University of California at Santa Cruz

Richard N. Cooper (chairman), Maurits C. Boas Professor of International Economics, Harvard University; Under Secretary of State for Economic Affairs, 1977–81

Jeffrey A. Frankel, Professor of Economics, University of California at Berkeley

Milton Friedman, Nobel Laureate in Economics; Senior Research Fellow, Hoover Institution, Stanford University

Randall Hinshaw, Professor of Economics Emeritus, The Claremont Graduate School

Otmar Issing, Member of the Board and of the Central Bank Council, Deutsche Bundesbank

Conrad C. Jamison, former Vice-President and Economist, Security Pacific National Bank

Christopher Johnson, Chief Economic Adviser, Lloyds Bank

Paul R. Krugman, Professor of Economics, Massachusetts Institute of Technology

Lionel W. McKenzie, Wilson Professor of Economics Emeritus, University of Rochester

Robert A. Mundell, Professor of Economics, Columbia University

John Rutledge, Chairman, Rutledge & Company, Inc.

Paul A. Samuelson, Nobel Laureate in Economics; Professor of Economics Emeritus, Massachusetts Institute of Technology

Robert Solomon, Guest Fellow, The Brookings Institution; former Adviser to the Board, Board of Governors of the Federal Reserve System

Thomas D. Willett, Horton Professor of Economics, The Claremont Graduate School and Claremont McKenna College

Foreword

In a period of convulsive global upheaval, marked by new hopes and new fears, a group of distinguished economists met in Claremont, California in late January 1991 for a two-day dialogue on international monetary issues in a rapidly changing world. Sponsored by the Claremont Graduate School in cooperation with the other Claremont Colleges, it was the sixth such meeting in Claremont since 1969 and the eleventh meeting in the "Bologna-Claremont" series on international economic problems, a project inaugurated in Italy in January 1967 at the Johns Hopkins University Bologna Center. Five of the conferences have taken place in Europe—three at the Bologna Center and two in Germany.

As at the other meetings, the dialogue was an off-the-cuff exchange of views among experts deliberately selected to reflect a wide range of viewpoints on topics that are often highly controversial. Over the years, this format has overwhelmingly demonstrated its success. Commenting on the procedure in his welcoming remarks to the participants of the 1977 Frankfurt conference, Karl Klasen, then the governor of the German central bank, said, "It is a distinct advantage that you have not prepared in advance a precise schedule and that, with one exception [the opening address of the moderator, the late Lord Robbins], you have no formal papers. This is a most creative formula for a successful meeting, and I am confident that in Frankfurt you will continue with distinction your tradition of stimulating brainstorming." That tradition has since continued, except that at the meetings since the Hamburg dialogue of 1980 the opening address has been omitted.

The 1991 conference took place in the midst of Operation Desert Storm, a few weeks before the end of that conflict. The Gulf War received some attention toward the end of the meeting, but was correctly interpreted as not likely to have lasting effects on international monetary arrangements. It did, however, have the unfortunate effect of causing the cancellation of the trip from Bologna to Claremont of Dr. and Mrs. Stephen Low. Dr. Low, the director of the Bologna Center, had planned to attend the conference as a ceremonial representative of the Center—a tradition established by the Center's founder and original director, Dr. C. Grove Haines, and his successor as director, Dr. Simon Serfaty.

Present or future Nobel laureates in economics have participated in most of the Bologna-Claremont dialogues. At the 1991 meeting, there were two: Milton Friedman and Paul A. Samuelson, the first American economist to receive the award. On the evening between the two days of the conference, Professor Samuelson delivered the second Robbins Memorial lecture, honoring the late Lord Robbins, who served with rare distinction as the moderator of seven of the dialogues. The public lecture, entitled "Economic Science Grapples with Dilemmas of International Finance," was delivered before a large audience and is reproduced at the end of this volume. The conference was honored by the presence of two representatives of the Robbins family: the Honorable Richard Robbins, the son of Lord and Lady Robbins, and Christopher Johnson, their son-in-law. Mr. Johnson, a leading British economist, was an eloquent participant in the dialogue.

The conference honored the late Francis Haynes Lindley (1899–1987), who for almost a half century was the president of the John Randolph Haynes and Dora Haynes Foundation, the chief source of financial support for the conference series. Mr. Lindley took a keen interest in the series, attending the meetings in Claremont as well as the 1971 Bologna conference and the 1977 Frankfurt dialogue. The 1991 conference was made possible by a generous grant from the Haynes Foundation. The Claremont Graduate School deeply appreciates the personal interest and involvement of F. Haynes Lindley, Jr., the foundation's president, and Paul A. Albrecht, who chairs its Committee on Research and Grants. Additional financial support was provided by Michael R. Harris, Pearl Hinshaw, Daniel C. Vandermeulen, and the Security Pacific Foundation.

A conference of this nature inevitably requires the assistance of a large number of people. Hearty thanks are due, first of all, to the distinguished participants, who interrupted busy schedules to come to Claremont—several from long distances, including two from Europe. For the third time, Professor Richard N. Cooper of Harvard University served superbly as chairman.

Premier thanks also go to Professor Randall Hinshaw, who has been the organizing force, the heart and soul, of this series. His unfailing commitment, his consummate leadership, and his unparalleled perseverance have kept the gatherings going. His vast experience, brought to bear on the 1991 meeting, made this perhaps the best yet.

As at the five earlier dialogues in Claremont, the sessions and luncheons took place on the charming campus of Scripps College. We owe much to Jo Ann Warner, the Scripps conference director, who went to great pains to assure ideal physical arrangements, and to Caroline Kroeker, the Scripps audio-visual coordinator, whose dedicated supervision resulted in a first-rate tape recording of the dialogue. Through the good offices of Professor Hans Palmer, who chairs its Department of Economics, Pomona College provided the auditorium for the Robbins Memorial Lecture.

As always, the staff of the Graduate School was helpful in many ways. To list all those who assisted would make this a much longer foreword, but one name in particular stands out: Luzma Brayton, the Graduate School's director of special events. With characteristic grace, skill, and enthusiasm, Mrs. Brayton devoted countless hours to the innumerable details involved in conference planning and in arranging the memorably delightful social functions. The smooth operation of the conference was also greatly assisted by Laurie Macaulay, director of the Graduate School Development Office, and her able staff, as well as by Alexander Huemer, a graduate student, who organized and supervised a highly efficient student taxi service for the participants.

In his foreword to the fifth volume in this series, my predecessor, Joseph B. Platt, raised the question: "What do these conferences and books accomplish?" He agreed with the answer provided by the late founding chairman, Willard L. Thorp, who at one of the early conferences stated that "there is no doubt in my mind that discussions among experts, including some in positions of special responsibility, cannot help but move us toward solutions."

The meetings in this series have been widely hailed for their warm and friendly spirit. Commenting on this aspect of the 1991 dialogue, Christopher Johnson wrote, "The conference was remarkably lively and good-humored. There was none of the bitterness sometimes found in other countries between economists of rival persuasions." Referring to his father-in-law, Lord Robbins, he added, "His spirit would have been pleased by this one." I most certainly believe it would!

John David Maguire
President
The Claremont Graduate School

Prologue

Randall Hinshaw

In January 1991, for the eleventh time during the past quarter century, a group of leading economists informally known as the "Bologna-Claremont" group met for a two-day dialogue on international economic problems. The meeting took place in Claremont, California, under the auspices of the Claremont Graduate School in cooperation with the other Claremont Colleges. Before commenting on that meeting, it may be helpful to the reader to provide some background on this long-standing conference series, which in certain respects has been unusual, if not unique.

Of the ten earlier meetings, five had taken place in Europe—three in Italy, two in Germany—and the other five in Claremont. The original conference, at the Johns Hopkins University Bologna Center in January 1967, was conceived as a one-time operation, but the format proved to be so attractive that the result was a series of exceptional longevity.

Several decisions were made at the outset. First, since the sole objective was the pursuit of truth, an effort would be made to invite participants who were known to hold widely differing views on the conference topic. Thus at the opening conference, on the role of gold in international monetary reform, all important points of view on this very controversial subject were ably represented.

Second, with the exception of the opening address of the moderator—a position which the eminent British economist, Lord Robbins, filled with great distinction for seven of the dialogues—there were to be no prepared papers. This was a clear break from the often boring standard academic conference format of prepared papers and prepared comments, with the papers frequently circulated in advance. Instead, the objective was to engage the participants in a lively off-the-cuff exchange of views, with no holds barred within the limits of civility. Far from generating ill temper, this procedure has resulted in meetings that have invariably been remarkably good-humored, with any barbs accompanied by smiles and laughter.

Third, it was agreed that there would be no conference report in the sense of a set of policy recommendations approved by the majority of conference members. Lord Robbins made this a condition of his participation, stating that, as moderator, he had no desire to be placed in the position of having to proclaim publicly why he disagreed with a particular formal recommendation. His decision on this matter, and of course his prestige as an economist and public figure, made it possible to attract economists of the highest distinction—individuals who otherwise would probably have turned down the invitation. Beginning with the first conference in 1967, in which Maurice Allais was a member, present or future Nobel laureates in economics have participated in most of the dialogues. At the 1991 meeting, there were two—Paul Samuelson and Milton Friedman, widely known for their policy disagreements—whose lively exchanges during the conference generated much good-hearted laughter, both from the participants and from the numerous student observers, for whom the event was a rare educational experience.

For each conference, an effort has been made to select the topic of foremost current concern. The concerns, of course, have changed considerably over the years. The 1967 Bologna conference on gold was followed by dialogues on the economics of international adjustment (Claremont, 1969), inflation as a global problem (Bologna, 1971), issues in international monetary reform (Claremont, 1973), stagflation (Claremont, 1975), domestic goals and financial interdependence (Frankfurt, 1977), international monetary anarchy (Claremont, 1978), global economic priorities (Hamburg, 1980), proposals for world economic recovery (Bologna, 1983), and issues connected with the U.S. dollar (Claremont, 1986).

The series has been blessed with two great chairmen: Willard L. Thorp, the distinguished economist and statesman, who chaired the first eight conferences, and Richard N. Cooper, the Maurits C. Boas Professor of International Economics at Harvard University, who has chaired the last three. Under the earlier regime, after the stage-setting opening address by Lord Robbins, Chairman Thorp, in consultation with the moderator and with the agreement of the other participants, worked out an agenda consisting of a small number of subtopics derived from the conference theme. The same procedure has been followed by Chairman Cooper, who, since the death of Lord Robbins in 1984, has combined the roles of chairman and moderator. Usually with only a few minutes notice, the chairman invites a participant with a particular interest in a given subtopic to introduce the discussion on that subject. The participants remain seated throughout the conference, and every effort is made to achieve spontaneity and to avoid the stodgy.

The conferences are recorded on tape, and a book has been derived from each meeting. Like the present volume, each book, apart from the introductory chapter, is a conservatively edited transcript of the conference tape recording. In a venture of this kind, there is always a temptation to rearrange the statements to achieve ideal coherence and order, but this can usually be done only by altering some of the language and possibly impairing the integrity of the dialogue. With only one exception, the lightly edited statements in this volume appear in the order in which they were made. Participants are given an opportunity to revise their statements, as submitted to them by the editor, but such revisions are always minor; for example, Professor Samuelson and Professor Krugman each changed only one word.

The theme of the 1991 dialogue was international monetary issues in a rapidly changing world. As Robert Mundell observed in his opening remarks, the words "rapidly changing" were almost an understatement of the situation. Completely unexpected momentous events had happened in the past three years: the end of the Berlin Wall and of a divided Germany, the liberation of the satellite countries of Eastern Europe, the collapse of Communism in the Soviet Union, and the end of the Cold War—all causes for joy in the west. But it was joy mixed with anxiety about whether Eastern Europe, with its heritage of centrally controlled economies and with its enormous inefficient bureaucracies, could make the tremendous adjustments necessary in moving toward market economies in a democratic setting without massive unemployment, major food shortages, and dangerous political turmoil. Unfortunately, that great champion and paragon of capitalism, the United States, was not functioning well as a role model for Eastern Europe, but was slipping into a serious and protracted recession.

The 1991 dialogue, as guided by Chairman Cooper, falls neatly into chapters. The chairman invited Robert Mundell to open the conference with a survey of current international monetary issues. Professor Mundell's able statement was followed by reactions from other participants, and on the basis of this discussion, the chairman proposed a provisional agenda. These statements form the content of chapter 1. The agenda concentrated on the economic problems of three regions: the United States (chapters 2 and 3); Western Europe, where attention was centered on the difficult monetary problems resulting from German unification (chapter 4) and on the movement toward Western European monetary integration (chapter 6); and Eastern Europe, where attention was directed to the issues facing both the former satellite countries and the now former Soviet Union (chapter 8). Also examined in the new setting was the case for the international coordination of economic policies (chapter 5) and the trend toward regional economic arrangements (chapter 7).

A feature of the two most recent conferences has been a public lecture honoring the late Lord Robbins, without whose participation in the formative years the series would never have taken place. The first of these lectures was delivered at the 1986 Claremont conference by Milton Friedman. At the 1991 meeting, the lecturer was Paul Samuelson. His lecture, entitled "Economic Science Grapples with Dilemmas in International Finance," appears at the end of this volume.

The 1991 conference took place during Operation Desert Storm, several weeks before the end of the Gulf War. While the conflict was very much in the minds of the participants, it was not discussed until toward the end of the dialogue, when Conrad Jamison made a statement about the possible implications. The chairman's prophetic "off-hand reaction" that the war still being fought was not likely to have a significant impact on international financial arrangements has been amply justified.

Nor have other momentous events in the months since the conference—notably the August 1991 coup and subsequent dissolution of the Soviet Union—significantly altered the nature of the problems and issues discussed in Claremont. The economic dilemmas facing the United States in dealing with unemployment, widespread poverty, sluggish growth, and the possibly reduced but perennial threat of inflation remain the same, as do the gargantuan economic problems facing Eastern Europe in its wrenching struggle away from centrally controlled economic systems toward workable and acceptable free-market arrangements in a democratic setting. As evidenced in the Maastricht agreement of December 1991, Western Europe continues to aspire toward economic and political union, with a timetable involving steps during the remaining 1990s toward a Western European central bank and a single Western European currency. The obstacles to such ambitious objectives are obvious, as demonstrated by the 1992 currency crises in the European Monetary System, and there is likely to be many a slip between cup and lip. But these are matters that are discussed at length in the ensuing chapters, and it would be redundant to pursue them further here.

So on with the dialogue.

1.

Exploration of the Issues

Introduced by Robert A. Mundell

Chairman Richard N. Cooper: For those of you to whom the Bologna-Claremont conferences are new and also for those who have been to them before, let me remind you that our format is really an open discussion of anything that we think is important, with special emphasis on international monetary issues, but interpreting that heading very broadly. So the agenda is for us to determine. We have asked Bob Mundell and Milton Friedman each to make a few remarks with a view to framing some items for discussion, and then, before we get into the discussion proper, I will ask others if they would like to add anything. After that, I will exercise my limited powers as chairman to try to group the topics so that we won't be going all over the place in every discussion. With that by way of general introduction, Bob, would you like to start us off?

Robert A. Mundell: Thank you, Richard. It's a great pleasure for me to be at this eleventh conference in the Bologna-Claremont series. Since the series started back in 1967, each conference has focused on the issues that seemed to be the most important at the time, as can be seen from the titles of the books that have been brought out and edited by Randall Hinshaw.

The theme of this conference is "international monetary issues in a rapidly changing world." I think the words "rapidly changing" almost understate the matter, because the changes that have occurred in the past two or three years have been far greater than anything that we've experienced in the preceding three decades. And these big changes—I think here of the changes in Eastern Europe as being the most important—include an acceleration of plans for the development of Western European monetary union and, after 1992, the acceleration of the agenda for the creation of a Western European currency. These issues are certainly going to dominate, and should dominate, much of our thinking at this meeting.

On the eastern front, the Eastern European countries and the Soviet Union face two broad sets of problems. One kind is macroeconomic, the other microeconomic. Each country faces the problem of stabilizing its currency. Currency stabilization may not mean the same

5

thing to Milton Friedman as to me, but it will certainly be an important ingredient in bringing the macroeconomic variables into line, as well as doing those things necessary for bringing the microeconomic system into order—through privatization, through tax reform, through deregulation, through changes in incentives, and so on. Eastern European countries will need to decide how far in the direction of market economies they are going to move and what will be the best path for achieving that goal.

Now on the Western European front, we could ask whether Western European monetary union is a desirable objective—whether it's desirable for Western Europe: for Europe as a whole, including Eastern Europe: for the world economy—and whether it's the best alternative. I think we should move inside the thinking of people in Western Europe to see if they are going to create a European currency. If so, what is the best way of going about it? And is time working on the side of monetary integration or against it? I think that if the opportunity for European monetary union isn't grasped soon, it will be lost; because with all the big changes that have been taking place, the one underlying current that I can see moving through these great upheavals is the trend toward a Europe of the nation state, more like the Europe of 1900 than the Europe of the 1970s, split by the Cold War and by the vast differences between the communist and the market economic systems. We should, however, think of what would be the best way of creating a European currency if that objective is to be achieved, and certainly with our friend from the Bundesbank here, this will be an excellent time to discuss that subject.

A third topic that we should not neglect in this group is the U.S. economy, which is moving into a recession. We need to think of what the long-run objectives should be for the U.S. economy, whether the present policy mix is correct, what the impact of the savings-and-loan crisis is, and the bearing of these internal matters on the position of the dollar, which is still the focus of the international monetary system.

The fourth subject that I suggest we should think about is the trend in the world toward regionalism—whether we want to see a world in which, as Europe moves toward its own integrated area, there are countervailing pressures for integration in other parts of the world. The United States and Canada, possibly joined by Mexico, may form another bloc, and is that trend a good thing or a bad thing for the world economy? More particularly, focusing on the international monetary system, if Western Europe does move toward a European currency, would we be better off by creating a truly international currency, or should we continue with the current system of rapidly changing exchange rates—a system that gave us a sharp depreciation of the dollar in the 1970s, a sharp appreciation in the early 1980s, and a sharp depreciation at the present time? Would it be better, instead of having these strong ups and down of the dollar, to have an international monetary system based either on fixed exchange rates or on some international monetary union, perhaps like Bretton Woods but without the defects that made Bretton Woods break down?

So these are the things that I think we should discuss: Eastern Europe, Western Europe, monetary union, the U.S. economy, regional problems of the world economy, and global monetary arrangements.

Milton Friedman: Bob has laid out a very broad agenda and a very good one. I'm going to pick up on one particular point within that agenda. I think a topic of special current interest and of great importance is the likely impact on the European Monetary System, over the next year or so, of what is happening in Germany. That's a bit oversimplified, because what I mean are the consequences of the changes in Eastern Europe, of which what's happening in Germany is simply a part.

You all know that I am not a great proponent of currency unions or of fixed exchange rates, but whether we like them or not, they have existed. The European Monetary System is fascinating as an intellectual subject, and we can understand it better if we recall the experience with the International Monetary Fund. In my view, the IMF worked quite well so long as the United States followed a relatively stable monetary policy on the one hand, and was willing on the other hand to be a kind of lender of last resort. In other words, the United States was willing to let other countries follow their own policies and to absorb the implications for capital flows. In the same way, in my opinion, the current European Monetary System has been working quite well—better than I would have expected—for the same reason: because the German central bank, the Bundesbank, has been following a relatively stable monetary policy and has been willing to be the absorber of last resort of the capital discrepancies.

The IMF broke down because the United States changed its policy in the 1960s. Partly under the pressure of the war, partly under the pressure of an attempt to broaden social policies, the United States wanted to expand more rapidly than was consistent with a stable monetary policy. It was able initially to export most of the inflation because of the IMF system, but that created an intolerable situation, and the system ultimately broke down. In the same way, what's happened in Eastern Europe and what's happened in Germany have, I think, introduced a similar kind of problem for the European Monetary System. Germany, as we all know, has been a large exporter of capital, and as I understand it—my neighbor here, Otmar Issing, can tell me whether I'm wrong—the bulk of that capital has been going to Common Market countries—50 percent to France and Spain and some part of the rest to other Common Market countries. Is that right?

Otmar Issing: Yes, that's true—for portfolio investment.

Friedman: And now, under the pressure from East Germany and under the pressure of demand from Eastern Europe, it looks very much as if Germany has a very strong incentive to shift from being a capital exporter to being a capital importer—or at least, if it continues to export capital, to export it to the Eastern European countries rather than to France and Spain and Britain to enable them to maintain overvalued currencies.

Now how does a country shift from being a capital exporter to being a capital importer? One way could be by inflation. Inflation would be equivalent to an appreciation of the mark, because it would make German goods more expensive. That is, a capital exporter is a country that is selling more than it is buying, and the way to reduce the outflow of goods is to make them more expensive. They can be made more expensive either by inflating internally or by appreciating the exchange rate. And here I've been saying that what I think is mainly going on is a fight between "P" and "K"—"P" standing for Poehl, the head of the Bundesbank, and "K" standing for Kohl, the Chancellor of Germany. The political pressures on Kohl will be to use the inflation route; the internal pressures on Poehl and the Bundesbank will be to try to maintain relatively stable prices, thereby driving up interest rates and the exchange rate.

Now if Germany were to choose the first route—inflation—that would in a way solve the problem for the neighboring countries without their having to change their nominal exchange rates. But if Germany chooses the second route, then it seems to me that there will be very great pressure on France, on Spain, and on Britain—particularly on Britain in view of the exchange rate at which it chose to tie into the European Monetary System. It seems to me to be an exchange rate that will be very hard to defend over any long period of time unless Britain achieves a much better record in cutting down its inflation than seems at all likely. Well, Christopher Johnson, who is here, may disagree with that.

Christopher Johnson: Yes, I certainly do unless you succeed in convincing me that I am wrong.

Friedman: At any rate, I offer this as a topic for us to discuss, because it seems to me that the change I've been describing—the process of Germany moving from a capital exporter to a capital importer or, at least, to a capital exporter elsewhere—is going to put a very severe strain on the current set of exchange-rate arrangements within the European Common Market. I have been expecting for a long time that sooner or later this system would break down anyway, just as I had predicted for many years that the IMF would break down. The EMS seems to me a fundamentally unstable arrangement. But it will be fascinating to see how the system develops under the new conditions and how that affects the European Common Market.

The extent to which countries are willing to make the necessary adjustments in their internal policies will, of course, have a great deal to do with the future prospects for what has been advertised as a common currency for Europe. I personally have long been very pessimistic, very negative, about achieving it. Bob mentioned one thing that is contradictory to a common currency, and that is the dominance of the nation state. I agree with him. We still have not gotten rid of nation states in Europe, and you cannot have a true common currency if you have more than one central bank.

Let me add a final comment. It's fascinating how the same things keep coming up in history over and over again. What I've been mentioning about the European Monetary System is really a replay of what was going on with the IMF in the 1960s.

Cooper: The strains on the Bretton Woods system.

Friedman: The strains on Bretton Woods. And what Bob was saying about the monetary problems of the United States—the banking system and the S&Ls—is a replay of the 1930s. In both cases, the same alternatives are being offered. In the 1930s, there was a 100 percent reserve banking plan known as the Chicago banking plan, and now the Brookings Institution and others are proposing what they're labeling the "narrow banking system," which is really a replay of the 100 percent reserve system. And in the international monetary area, the alternatives that were proposed in the Bretton Woods case—the restructuring of exchange-rate arrangements or floating exchange rates—are the same alternatives that are being proposed now. So history has something to teach us.

Robert Solomon: It occurs to me that we could broaden Milton's proposal a little beyond the short-term implications of what's happening in Germany. He started with the proposition that Germany will switch from being a capital exporter to being a capital importer; its current-account surplus will disappear. We might examine the question that a number of people have raised recently. After we move out of the present slowdown, will the world be facing some sort of shortage of saving—saving to which Germany, with its current-account surplus, has been contributing in the past? That would be a longer-term aspect of Milton's question.

And then perhaps also, as an agenda item that in my view ought to underlie the topics raised by both Bob and Milton, I think we should acknowledge—particularly in a conference that is a continuation of conferences organized by Randall over the past quarter of a century— at least one important way in which the world has changed since these meetings began. And the way I have in mind at the moment, because it's most relevant to how international monetary arrangements now work, is the enormous increases in the mobility of capital. That feature was not present when Randall organized his first conference, and it has implications for almost every topic that has been suggested by Bob and Milton.

Paul R. Krugman: Before talking about policy issues, we might want to talk a little bit about the way the world works. It seems to me that we're bound to be talking at cross purposes as this discussion goes on, because of fundamental disagreements about the way the mechanism operates. We can't really talk sensibly about a policy issue regarding Europe without some underlying model of how international macroeconomics plays out. And we ought to spend a little time talking about what we've learned from the past fifteen years or so.

Let me just put that in a bit of context and leave it. Suppose that one had gathered a group like this before it actually began gathering— let's say in the late 1940s. I think most of the people would have held that prices were sticky, were difficult to change, and at the same time felt that adjustments in relative prices were very important to deal with changes in the world, with changes in competitiveness. As a result, it would have been argued that exchange-rate changes were very important; adjustability of exchange rates was a valuable thing. On the other hand, financial markets in general and exchange markets in particular were regarded as unreliable and speculative, not to be trusted, which meant that flexible exchange rates were a mixed blessing and far from problem-free. That was, in a way, the underlying basis of the Bretton Woods arrangements.

I think that fifteen years ago—I don't know what actually went on here in these conferences—but fifteen or even ten years ago, there would have been people saying, Well, we now understand financial markets, we understand rational expectations, and there isn't any problem with financial markets as long as policies are stable. And we also understand that all that Keynesian stuff about sticky prices is wrong and that anticipated shocks have no effect on employment. Maybe it's all actually just real shocks anyway, and therefore there is neither very much cost to having exchange rates free to float nor much benefit from adjusting them.

My view, with which some of you here may disagree, is that the evidence of the past fifteen years has accumulated to the point that we now know that a late-1940s view of the system is essentially right— that markets, speculative markets in general and exchange markets in particular, have behaved just as badly as their critics, such as John Maynard Keynes, might have expected and that prices have been remarkably sticky. The correlation between nominal and real exchange-rate changes is higher than anyone—even the most rabid neo-Keynesian— might have suggested. We need to be clear about what our conceptual basis is before we discuss these policy issues.

Jeffrey A. Frankel: Perhaps our agenda is already too crowded, but I will offer one possible addition, international macroeconomic policy coordination, a subject that is obviously tied to some of the issues on exchange rates and other things that we've been discussing. It is rather striking that in the early 1980s there were many economists who taught that policymakers were needlessly giving up a possible advantage— that by pursuing policies cooperatively, we could do better. To some extent, with a lot of fanfare, that process was tried at the Plaza in 1985. Now, six years later, the Group of Seven are still meeting, but there was a meeting lately that made very little news. I guess every meeting has followed a downward trend in how much attention it received. So we could ask, Is that deserved? Is coordination dead? Or, perhaps, did it never really happen? And, what do we think should happen in the future with the G-7?

Solomon: Jeff suggested that economic policy coordination be put on the agenda, and I certainly second that suggestion. But he put it in the context of the Plaza agreement, and the implication seemed to be that economic policy coordination is aimed at exchange-rate stabilization. I think we ought to think of that concept much more broadly—as Jeff does in his writings—as having the broader purpose of improving macroeconomic performance in the world economy, not just stabilizing exchange rates.

Frankel: Absolutely, yes.

Cooper: Let me now try to organize our discussion. I propose that we start out with the near-term issues, with a one- to two- or three-year horizon. I am thinking of the issues Bob Mundell raised about the U.S. economy and the issues that Milton raised in connection with Europe. I suggest that we then turn to what I consider the longer-term issues, such as the prospects for, or desirability of, a full monetary union in Western Europe, or substitute arrangements, and the trends toward regionalism in the world economy that have monetary or currency aspects, but also a trade dimension.

I think we should devote some time to currency arrangements in Eastern Europe, one of Bob Mundell's topics. How should the Eastern European countries, all of which until a few years ago started from a position of central planning, in which the monetary system played only a fringe role in the functioning of the economy, switch from that position to one in which the monetary system plays a central role? That seems to me a fascinating issue for monetary economists to consider.

Among the longer-run issues, we should address Bob Solomon's question about the shortage of savings. My working assumption as an economist has been that there always has been a shortage of savings and that there always will be in some sense; so when one talks about a looming shortage of savings, this must mean something different from the general shortage of savings and the fact that resources are scarce. I take it that Bob meant to pose this, not as a problem in a year in which the United States is slipping into recession, but as a longer-term issue for the 1990s.

Is what I have suggested an agreeable procedure? We start out with a one- to three-year horizon, with the focus on the United States and on Germany this morning; move from there into some discussion of policy coordination; and then, having exhausted ourselves on those issues, address the questions of European monetary union and regionalism, reserving time (perhaps tomorrow afternoon) for Eastern European developments and for what our advice to those countries might be as they try to create a tabula rasa.

2.

U.S. Issues: Ten Views

Introduced by Milton Friedman

Chairman Cooper: We start now with the United States. Who would like to begin the discussion on the relatively near-term prospects for the United States and what they portend for the rest of the world? Milton?

Friedman: I want to start out by giving a background fact—just a fact. I think it's a fascinating fact. The average ex post long-term real interest rate in the United States for a hundred years, as measured by Anna Schwartz and myself in our book *Monetary Trends*, was 3.29 percent. In the period from 1960 to 1980, the average ex post real exchange rate in the United States was 1.2 percent. In the decade 1980 to 1990, measured the same way, it was 6.3 percent.

Cooper: Now just so we're clear on the measure you're giving us, is this the 30-year government bond rate, say, divided by . . .

Friedman [interrupting]: For the 100-year figure, it's corporate bonds. But from the 1960s to the 1990s, it's the 30-year government bond rate minus that year's rate of change in the GNP deflator.

Cooper: In the deflator, not the consumer price index?

Friedman: Not the CPI; the deflator. The result is an ex post short-run real measure, and it's obviously a combination of mistaken anticipations about what inflation's going to be—obviously too low when inflation was going up and too high when inflation was coming down. And the reason I mention it as background is that I think it guides directly to Bob Solomon's point, because what he's asking is whether we are going to see a long-term upward shift in the real interest rate. Bob, is that your question?

Solomon: That's another way of asking it, surely.

Cooper: Let me ask Milton about a different measure, since I don't like the measure that he just gave us; it seems to me to confuse the long run and the short run. What is the real rate of interest on 30-year bonds? Actually, we have no more recent observations than 30 years ago—that is to say, the 30-year bond rate in 1960, adjusted for the change in the price level between 1960 and 1990 as measured, for example, by the GNP deflator. That seems to me a more accurate measure of the long-term real interest rate, and I guess it's a calculation that would be worth doing. Maybe Jeffrey has done it.

Frankel: The movements are so striking that it doesn't really matter how you measure it.

Cooper: But the last figure Milton gave us was for the 1980s, which, I would argue, can't be measured yet. The most recent available figure for the 30-year real interest rate in my measure—the figure for 1960—would actually, I think, be negative. And we don't know what the 30-year real interest rate for 1990 will be until the year 2020, which is a long time from now.

Frankel: But that can't be what we're trying to get at. It's possible to make an estimate without waiting 30 years. I've used projections forecasting future inflation rates based on past inflation.

Cooper: But Milton was clear on ex post.

Friedman: Let me add one more fact that is deeply fascinating. If you look at a chart, year to year, using real rates as I have defined them, for the period from 1875 until now, you will find that they are strikingly different before and after 1960–65. Before 1960, the nominal long-term rate moves very slowly because you are on a commodity standard and everybody expects that upward and downward movements in the price level will average out, as they did most of the time. And so nobody paid any attention to the short-term movements. The nominal long-term rate was essentially the ex ante real rate. In the period from 1960–65 on, the nominal rate and the ex post real rate are about equally smooth. The behavior is absolutely striking; it's a wholly different relation. We're in a new monetary world, and now people are no longer basing their behavior on those very long-term judgments.

Cooper: On nominal rates?

Friedman: On nominal rates.

Cooper: Oh, I agree with that. But the ex post real rates in my concept—that is to say, with a 30-year holding period—were actually quite variable in the nineteenth century.

Friedman: Oh, very.

Cooper: The nominal rates were stable. Now the question we can't answer is whether the ex post real rates on a 30-year holding period have more or less instability than in the nineteenth century. We know the nominal rates have become much more variable.

Friedman: No, they have a different trend; they're not more variable.

Cooper: They've had higher variability as well as an upward trend, so that bond markets have become more like the stock market in a sense.

Friedman: And these short-term ex post real rates have become much more stable.

Cooper: Okay, then that's a fact—an alleged fact.

Friedman: A fact very relevant to the question we're debating.

Cooper: Paul Samuelson would like to say something.

Paul A. Samuelson: Yes, I have some questions. When Bob Solomon speaks of a possible new shortage of savings in the future, I naturally take a non–Wall Street viewpoint about this.

Solomon: In contrast to me?

Samuelson: No, no; let my contrast develop. I take a Paul Douglas or Robert Solow or Edward Denison view of what is the good in an economic system—as far as its future consumption possibilities are concerned—of forgoing present consumption and increasing an increment of capital formation. I think that how a bond portfolio has fared in a particular decade in terms of the cost of living is more of a Wall Street consideration.

I'm going to put this in the form of a question. As we put together all of the guesses about what Denison's studies will show and what Solow's studies will show in the future, do we have the impression that there was a sea change on the upside in the real marginal productivity of thrift in the 1980s? Or, as has been suggested, has this something to do with the usual seesaw of expectations after an inflation trend has been replaced by a different inflation trend and as people in Wall Street and Main Street are getting used to it? I have to say that my initial impression, not having gone beyond the back of an envelope, is that there has not been, for the world as a whole, a notable increase in the marginal productivity of capital in this period.

Krugman: Let me tell you what people I've talked to on Wall Street— investment bankers—say, which I think makes all this even more puzzling, and it bears on the capital-shortage issue. They say, Well, what we feel is that during the 1980s capital was abundant, but it's going to be scarce in the 1990s. In view of Milton Friedman's facts, that's a very peculiar thing to say about the 1980s. I suggest that what people are talking about in this connection has nothing to do with the real interest rate or with any measure of the real interest rate. The stories we hear about the future capital shortage, all of which I find dubious in a macroeconomic sense, have to do with the projected capital needs of Eastern Europe, where I find that people who emphasize the international considerations don't have a sense of how small international capital flows are, relative to world saving and investment.

I think that what is really going on here is the concerns of Wall Street, not about savings or investment, but about the availability of certain kinds of capital. What the Wall Street people really are talking about is the drying up of capital for highly leveraged transactions—about the end of the era of high leverage and the abundant capital for certain kinds of risk-taking which was available during the 1980s. They're really talking about the fall of Michael Milken in a sense rather than about the capital needs of Eastern Europe.

Friedman: I think what you're saying is right, but it's only part of the story. What we're talking about is the rate of interest that people think they'll have to pay when they borrow capital and the rate of return they think they can earn by using it. Now what happened during the 1980s could have happened only if people had assumed that they would be able to repay at much lower real rates. And because they thought that they could pay at low real rates, they were more than willing to borrow capital, and it was wasted. It was spent on projects that should never have been undertaken, and they would not have been undertaken if people had not grossly underestimated the real interest rate that they were in fact going to have to pay on those projects.

Now that gets into a very complicated case. Paul Samuelson's point is right; the real return on physical capital hasn't really changed. Maybe all that's happened is that some people have lost money and some people have made money. But the physical assets that have been created are still yielding a kind of marginal return that you can expect over a very long period of time. The market is stupid; it's not smart from a long-run point of view. It takes a long time for the market to adjust to a fundamental change in the direction of inflation. And so the 1980s were a period when people thought the upswing would continue indefinitely, and the result was, I think, a very large waste of capital, reflected in part in the savings-and-loan situation, in the bad bank loans, and so on. So there were very real effects; it wasn't only a Wall Street phenomenon.

Krugman: There were certainly some people who did not realize that inflation was coming down on a sustained basis, but there was also a very heavy element of style of lending, writ much larger than just in the S&Ls. A major reason that companies were willing to pay these rates was that they were playing a heads-we-win, tails-you-lose game, and a major reason that funds were made available was that there was a heavy pushing of the downside risk onto the taxpayer, either explicitly or implicitly. We're just beginning to realize the extent to which that happened during the 1980s. A lot of what went on had nothing to do with the physical productivity of capital or with technology decisions; it had to do with the quite correct appreciation that it was possible, in taking risks, to take the option value of the upside for yourself and put the downside onto the general public.

Mundell: Well, I think a factor that dominated the 1930s was the very substantial revolution in tax rates. This certainly raised the after-tax marginal efficiency of capital.

Cooper: Paul Samuelson made a distinction that I think we ought to get on the table, and it relates to the issue that Paul Krugman raised earlier about how the world works. In assessing the real rate of return to capital, is there a difference between the United States, or North America, and the rest of the world? Is it possible or likely that one of the things that's happened over the last 30, 50, or even 100 years—to take Milton's data—is that the world is more integrated than it was, so that one can see simultaneously a rise in the real rate of returns to capital in the United States and a decline elsewhere in the world, with no change in the overall average? I'm talking about real capital now— not the Wall Street version—in the United States and in the rest of the world, as compared with, let us say, 30 years ago.

Friedman: I don't know about 30 years ago, but I question your assumption that the world is more integrated today in terms of long-term capital than it was 100 years ago. I think it's quite the opposite. A century ago, you could have long-term international investment on a large scale. British capital built railroads in the United States, in Argentina, and elsewhere. When people talk about this great increase in the mobility of capital, they're talking about short-term capital—very short-term. In my opinion, there has been no increase in the mobility of long-term capital. Maybe I'm wrong—and this is a fact that can be investigated—but I think it's very dubious that there has been an increase in the mobility of long-term capital. In recent years, we have had some direct investment by Japan and Britain in the United States, but look at how hard it is for any of the developing countries around the world to get long-term capital from abroad, and compare this with what happened in the nineteenth and early twentieth centuries when long-term capital flowed from Germany and France into Africa, and British capital flowed into China and elsewhere. You don't have an economic phenomenon like that today.

Frankel: There are many different possible definitions of international capital mobility. Let me suggest one clear measure by which capital mobility has increased very steadily over the last 20 years, and I suspect that it is higher than it was 100 years ago—namely, short-term covered interest differentials, the differentials falling for the United States and Germany, and then during the 1980s, for Britain, Japan, France, and Italy as they removed their capital controls.

Now a distinction that is commonly made—and that has been made here—is that short-term capital is highly mobile, but long-term capital is not. I think maybe that's not exactly the right place to draw the distinction. I would suggest that the distinction should be, not between the short term and the long term, but between financial or nominal capital and real capital. It is harder to do tests of covered interest parity going out to longer terms, but you can do it. You can use swap data on Eurobonds, and that sort of data suggests that for 20-year bonds or 30-year bonds, the barriers to capital movement across national borders are almost as small as for the short term.

A measure of capital mobility that does not show a big change or, if anything, a change in the wrong direction is real interest differentials. Over the past decade these are as large as, or larger than, they were in earlier years.

Krugman: What we know is that any measure of economic integration we can use shows a big U shape over the past 80 years—not a steady progress toward greater world integration. There was a steady disintegration of the world economy during the period between 1913 and the early postwar years, which tells us right away that technology does not drive the system. There may be long-term technological trends, but they can be overridden very easily by the political environment. Most measures of trade suggest that the world is somewhat more integrated now than it was in 1913, but not dramatically so.

On the other hand, looking at net flows of resources, we got very excited when Japan ran current-account surpluses in the vicinity of 4 percent of gross national product for about two years. And of course those surpluses have now faded away quite rapidly. Yet the United Kingdom ran an average current-account surplus of 5 percent per year for 40 years before World War I. So the magnitude of international transfers of capital that we saw in the late nineteenth and early twentieth centuries was on a scale that is unthinkable today.

Johnson: Paul has just made the point that I was going to make—that certainly in relative terms the scale of capital exports, notably by the United Kingdom (I don't have figures for other countries), was quite enormous before the First World War. Much of it was private portfolio and direct investment, and it was either in colonial areas or what one might call the neocolonial areas of Latin America, where the risks were judged to be bearable and the capital was, in fact, productively invested.

What I really wanted to say was that we seem to have departed a long way from the model we all used to have in the 1960s—that, on the whole, the industrial countries would tend to have balance-of-payments surpluses and would be the natural capital exporters of the world, while the developing countries would be the natural capital importers. Now this model is all over the place. Germany and Japan are capital exporters, but the United States is one of the world's biggest capital importers. Mexico in some years has been a capital exporter, and I wonder whether one can just regard these positions, which do shift quite rapidly, as being a kind of random residual error in the way the world economy is run, or rationalize it by saying, Well, the investment opportunities in the United States are better than they are, let us say, in Argentina. And the ultimate logic of this is that the United States will attract not only capital but population, as it has been doing. It has an environment for productive investment which doesn't exist in the developing countries. So I think there are a lot of questions here which I won't even try to answer.

Solomon: Having introduced the notion that we should keep in mind increasing capital mobility, let me just say what I was thinking when I said that. Milton may be right if we take a long-term view; I don't know whether capital is more mobile or less mobile now than it was in the nineteenth century. But I think what's relevant for this conference, which is going to be discussing international monetary arrangements, is to compare the present situation, not with the nineteenth century, but with, say, the 1950s and 1960s. What matters is the change from the latter period, and I think we could all agree that, as compared with the fifties and sixties, we have much greater capital mobility today. That's all we need for the purpose of this conference.

Cooper: I would just add to that point. It's not only for international monetary arrangements but for the framing of economic policy at the national level, which for the last half century has been very different from what it was in the nineteenth century. The way national governments now think about framing economic policy was unknown, or almost unknown, in the late nineteenth cventury.

Solomon: Absolutely.

Thomas D. Willett: When we get into the issue of savings rates and related questions, it is real capital mobility that's important. All the studies that I've seen give the same general conclusions that Jeff Frankel and Paul Krugman mentioned—that there's a much lower degree of mobility for real capital than for financial capital. But the degree of financial capital mobility, I think, is not as great as Jeff appears to conclude, because the deviations from covered interest parity don't really give us a good measure of that. I do think we can infer from the movements in covered arbitrage that we have a lot fewer capital controls today than we had 20 years ago, and I agree that financial capital mobility in the quantitative sense has certainly increased, but I don't think we have a really good measure yet of how big that increase is.

Issing: Let me raise a question on a subject on which there is much concern in Europe, especially among central banks—namely, the so-called credit crunch in the United States. If one looks at Milton Friedman's figures, one wouldn't expect a credit crunch. In an integrated world capital market, foreign capital would come in at these high real interest rates, so you couldn't have this special credit shortage.

Samuelson: No, it's a qualitative credit crunch in which the medium-sized businesses and small-sized businesses report that creditworthy loan applications that were honored in the past are now refused. Now it's unthinkable that a foreign profit-seeking capitalist would fill that gap, because it's completely shot through with localized information. A foreigner would be in the worst position to decide which of these credit applications were truly creditworthy and which were not.

Friedman: Just a word on interest rates. Interest rates are composed of two parts, the real part and the inflation part. I think that there is reason to believe that the inflation rate is coming down sharply; it has been declining for the last two or three years, and I believe this trend is going to continue in 1991 and 1992. So I think that U.S. domestic interest rates are going to decline rather sharply. Now this doesn't preclude a credit crunch of the kind that Paul is talking about.

Lionel W. McKenzie: I would like to broaden the discussion a bit. We have heard a number of remarks today about appealing to the empirical record to discover what model is correct or to estimate the parameters of the model one thinks will serve best. I rather wonder how much weight economic statistics can bear in making these decisions. I recall a previous president of the American Statistical Association once saying that he had never seen economic statistics that were any good. He gave as an example the balance of trade between the United States and Canada, and he was not at all sure that we knew whether the balance of trade of the United States with Canada was in surplus or in deficit. So it seems to me that this is an important question.

Now of course financial statistics collected by central banks are presumably much more reliable than statistics of exports and imports. On the other hand, I recall my old professor at Princeton, Oskar Morgenstern, being very skeptical about some of the financial statistics and saying that they might be erroneous by at least 15 percent. So I simply ask to what degree this hampers our attempt to decide between models on the basis of available statistics or to fit data to models by econometric means to try to determine what their parameters are.

Cooper: I just want to report, since you may not know, that we've now solved the problem of U.S.-Canadian trade statistics. For years there was a big discrepancy between what the Canadians reported and what we reported. That problem has now gone away because we simply adopted the Canadian statistics. We decided that they were better than ours, so we've now officially adopted them.

Mundell: Just a word on the Canadian statistics. One of the big problems in calculating things is that when Canada moved to a floating exchange rate in the 1950s, Canadian companies submitted their reports in American dollars, and the Canadian government didn't realize this.

Krugman: I want to be clear about what kind of evidence at least I'm appealing to. It mostly involves exchange rates, which I think we do know, and price indices that are not perfect but, I think, are not subject to radical year-to-year changes in the extent of error. As far as I'm concerned, the basic facts that are crucial to deciding what kind of model to use are that there's essentially a near-perfect correlation between nominal exchange-rate changes and real exchange-rate changes, which involves only exchange-rate and price-index data, and that forward exchange rates have no predictive power over future changes in exchange rates. Whether we think our trade figures are really good— and we know that they aren't—it's clear that when you have large movements of relative prices of 20 or 30 percent, you do not get instantaneous large shifts of consumption and production from one country to another. I don't need to believe that the trade statistics are precise evidence to see that. So we're not talking about fine points here; we're talking about gross features of experience, which do not really depend on the data being the most wonderful stuff in the world.

Mundell: Quickly, on the exchange rate, the correlation between real and nominal exchange rates for the U.S. dollar is very high: I agree with that. But as you move away to other countries, it gets worse and worse. The correlation between real and nominal exchange rates is exceptionally strong for the United States but not for other countries, and for a lot of small countries it doesn't exist at all.

Johnson: Let me make one more point about statistics, which is that in the kind of economic and monetary union proposed in Europe, once we've cleared away the customs posts, there will be no agency to collect trade statistics within the area. We shall try to measure them by surveys, but we will not, in effect, be getting the kind of signals for policy that we get now from the trade numbers, and it will therefore be assumed that, whatever the trade balance is, it will be compensated by banking and investment flows, which is what happens within the United States. And that might bring us to the problem of regions.

Krugman: One of the theories about why international capital mobility, in the sense of actually transferring resources, was higher before World War I than it has been at any time since is that in those days countries did not publish balance-of-payments statistics.

Johnson: Exactly.

Friedman: That's a very real problem in this country, where there is all the talk about the United States being a major debtor nation. I used to say to people in California that if they had the statistics they would know that California is a major debtor country—that, probably, taken as a country, California is more in debt externally than the United States as a whole. I know that, because interest rates in California have been higher than interest rates in New England for about a hundred years now. That can only mean that capital has been flowing one way. Suppose the headline in the newspaper tomorrow were to be that California is a major debtor state to the tune of $10 trillion or whatever it is. Could the governor refrain from doing anything about it?

Cooper: And if he decided he couldn't, what then?

Friedman: That goes back to another element about statistics. Our interests as economists and our interest in policy may sometimes run in opposite directions. I once had a talk in Hong Kong with Sir John Cowperthwaite when he was Hong Kong's financial secretary. He said, "You know, these civil servants of mine want to compute GNP statistics for Hong Kong. But I'm not going to let them do that. If they do that, they'll want to use them!"

Solomon: Speaking of statistics, since the record shows that we're talking about the United States as a net debtor, the record also ought to show that the official statistics that are published greatly exaggerate our net debtor position.

Krugman: And even the direction.

Solomon: Well, possibly the direction, but certainly the size. The official statistics underestimate the value of U.S. assets abroad by an enormous amount.

3.

U.S. Monetary and Fiscal Dilemmas and Options

Introduced by Paul A. Samuelson

Chairman Cooper: I have asked Paul Samuelson to begin the discussion on the present state of the U.S. economy.

Samuelson: On August 1, 1990, the experts were all pretty much in agreement that the economy was in a soft landing within a growth recession. About half of them thought it would be an actual recession, and about half thought we would luck through. By August 3, that question was resolved because of the invasion of Kuwait, with a plunge in consumer confidence and a traditional supply-side shock from the increase in the price of oil—a much weaker supply-side shock than we had in the 1970s. The expectation from the White House was that this would be a mild recession—that by the middle of the year we would have hit bottom and would come up.

The trouble in the Middle East has complicated that picture, and the consensus forecasters believe that if this is a short war with a happy outcome, it will reverse most of the effects that took place between August 1 and August 3. But there is a respectable minority who think that what's going on in the way of weakness in this period will leave its mark on the few hundred more banks that are extremely likely to fail—that we have a qualitative Hyman Minsky kind of credit overlay of problems here—and that if the war is an unpleasant war before it involves a lot of spending on military equipment, that will be an adverse factor. Everybody has regarded Japan and Germany as the strong locomotives in this particular period, and the hope and expectation has been that the United States will benefit from the past weakness of the dollar and that exports will be one of the elements of strength. Of course, to the degree that the supply shock again becomes important, it's a worldwide thing and a depressant on other countries. I hope that's a fair summary.

Cooper: Thank you, Paul. Maybe I should ask the group, What, if anything, do you think we should do? Let's stipulate that we're in a recession. I guess it's official now; the National Bureau of Economic Research has declared a recession or has just declared that it is going to declare a recession.

Frankel: It wasn't an official declaration.

Cooper: No, it was a forecast of their own future behavior.

Samuelson: The actual announcement from the Mount was that we have had a telephone conference and we think the likelihood is such that, at a later date, there will be declared to have been a recession. The problem is complicated by the fact that not only must you predict the present you must also predict the last few months. To decide whether we are in a recession, using the typical criteria to define a recession, you must really predict that the quarter that is not yet over— it won't be over for two more months—is going to be a down quarter. And the latest report of a 2.1 percent decline in the fourth quarter of 1990 was actually a cheerful report in comparison with what the consensus forecasters had expected.

Friedman: I might say that, as a National Bureau veteran who has made a great deal of use of the National Bureau cycle arrangements, I think the National Bureau definition of a recession is not a very useful definition. I think it's absurd to let anything whatsoever depend on whether the economy is growing at 0.1 percent per year or declining at 0.1 percent per year. The concept of a growth recession, which Paul spoke of, is a much more meaningful one. The average growth rate of the U.S. economy for 100 years has been 3 percent a year. We've been below 2 percent in real growth since the middle of 1989, and I think we've been in a recession in any meaningful sense since then.

I think it was deepened in the last few months by what Paul spoke of—the war—but also by the fact that the Federal Reserve made its usual mistake, when it operates through interest rates, of not moving fast enough when circumstances are changing fast. The Fed didn't drive down interest rates fast enough to enable the money supply to increase. And the Federal Reserve authorities were somewhat confused by the very, very strange and atypical behavior of currencies as a result of developments in Eastern Europe, so that it looked as if the monetary base was going up, but it really wasn't. Reserves weren't rising. And I believe that in the last three months the monetary growth rate has been much lower than the Fed intended it to be or than was desirable—not necessarily from a cyclical point of view but from a secular one.

Samuelson: If I could now give some . . .

Cooper [interrupting]: Normative views?

Samuelson: Right. I'm a Federal Reserve activist—not a simple rules person; you must make allowances for that. I think that the Fed has been a little bit late and a little bit skimpy in this particular period for a variety of reasons, some of them excusable and some less excusable. For one thing, there are 18 people who vote—not at any one time, but they're in the panel to vote—and I think there are about four or five of them who take seriously the task of achieving a stable price level by 1995. And although they don't even reveal it to their spouses, in their heart of hearts they really want a little recession. In willing the ends, they must will the means, so they always find every reason for acting slowly. The other thing is that, with supply shocks, it is always difficult to run an economy.

But the third thing—and it's very relevant to our discussion—is that the Federal Reserve, being the central bank of a nation that accounts for 22 percent of global output, is quite constrained in the present period by international considerations. I don't mean that it couldn't punch its way through those constraints, but there really is a constraint that Paul Volcker did not have in the middle of 1982. In the middle of 1982, the dollar was uncharacteristically strong; he didn't have to worry about the gnomes of Zurich, and he didn't have to worry that people in Wall Street would think him soft on inflation. He could make a shrewd guess that they would welcome his intervention, and from the first sign of the maneuver, it was embraced by Wall Street. It worked like a charm.

This is not the situation that faces Chairman Greenspan. In terms of where nominal interest rates have been and where they are now, the United States comes into this period with low real interest rates— not high real interest rates. And so, when the Federal Reserve listens to sirens like me and becomes more activist, it must realize that this is going to have an effect upon the foreign-exchange markets—to have the dollar go down—which perturbs me extremely little, but perturbs many people in the establishment quite a lot. Finally, let me say that I think Alan Greenspan is a very savvy person, but I think in this period he's lost his touch a little bit.

Cooper: If I can interpret your agreeing with Milton that the Fed ought to ease now, I'm going to ask you the harder question—by how much? Getting the right direction is fairly easy.

Samuelson: Before we make too much of my agreement with Milton [prolonged laughter], I agreed with the Fed that it should get off the course of monetarism in 1982, declare a victory over inflation, and all the rest; now, in my opportunistic way, I am joining Milton. I want the Fed to return to the course of monetarism because it's going to fry my fish in this particular period. So we'll march along together.

Cooper: For a while [more laughter].

Friedman: We always march along together when the Fed has been abnormally low in creating money, and we always march differently when the Fed has been abnormally high.

Cooper: I don't want this question of how much monetary expansion to be forgotten, but Bob Mundell has asked for the floor.

Mundell: I agree that the Fed has erred somewhat on the side of being too cautious, but if it weren't for another problem. I would take Paul's remarks very seriously with respect to the foreign-exchange market. I think there are definite limits on the extent the Fed can expand without causing chaos in the foreign-exchange market, and I would be among those people who think it would be very damaging in the long run for the United States to let the dollar go down sharply. Now, on the other hand, the longer-run issue that faces the banking system—the state of asset prices and so on—does lead me to the view that we're in for somewhat more inflationary policies over the next few years just because of the state of the banking system. I think it's inevitable that we'll have to move in that direction to some extent, though I'm very unhappy about it.

But what should we do in the middle of a recession when there are limits on what we can do in easing monetary policy without inviting a collapse of the dollar? This is where I think we need another instrument of policy. Back in the late 1970s and early 1980s, we could have tight money and combine that with a big tax cut—a policy that had pros and cons, though it was definitely possible at that time. But for probably both economic and political reasons, now it is not possible to have a generalized tax cut such as occurred in the early Reagan years.

However, one particular kind of tax change could be taken, which would have a very positive and strong effect on the economy, and that is a cut in taxes on capital gains. I think that the United States is suffering severely in international competition because of our very heavy taxes on capital gains and that we would gain a great deal economically by reducing them.

Now there are different ways of doing that. We could cut the actual rate. There's a strong argument for that, and I'll come to it in a moment. Another possibility would be to index the capital-gains tax, so that we don't have an increase in taxes just because of an inflationary monetary system. That consideration may become more and more important, to the extent that a more inflationary stance may be necessary because of the state of the banking system. Now even if we index the capital-gains tax rate—and many agree that we should, including the *New York Times*, certainly a Democratic paper—this is not enough, because, first of all, there would be no offsets of capital losses against capital gains. So on that ground alone, there should be a lower tax on capital gains. This seems to me the one single policy that would be very beneficial on the fiscal side and that would help us get out of the recession and back into a renewed growth phase in the 1990s.

Krugman: One first comment. Since Bob Mundell says we need some kind of fiscal expansion, let me make a proposal that of course wouldn't possibly be adopted. Instead of a tax cut, how about a spending increase, at about $600 million a day, and since the problem is very regional, is very concentrated—especially in New England—how about a spending increase that is especially oriented toward high-technology manufacturing?

Mundell: That's a Keynesian solution. But my tax cut is a supply-side fiscal expansion; it's not a Keynesian remedy.

Cooper: If I may say so, it is not satisfactory to reject an argument simply by labeling it. You have to tell us why.

Mundell: If Paul allows me, I will. It's my belief that remedies that require internal financing don't have any multiplier effect; they have a zero multiplier effect because the increase in spending is completely offset by the financing. On the other hand, a cut in the capital-gains tax would have a once-for-all positive revenue effect, and at the same time would raise the marginal efficiency of capital. These are policy effects that an increase in government spending wouldn't have.

Krugman: All right; let me just say that we certainly have a difference in models here. I don't think I quite understand the model that Bob is advancing, but I certainly wouldn't agree with it if I did understand it.

Friedman: How can you disagree with it if you don't understand it?

Krugman: Well, because the model I believe in gives me a different answer.

Friedman: You mean that whatever he says is wrong whether you understand it or not?

Krugman: Well, Bob certainly didn't say what I say—which is right. Sorry. Let me go back to something else. There is a very important link between what Milton Friedman brought up at the very beginning and what Paul Samuelson was saying about the international dimension. We're in a situation where Germany, for reasons having to do with the reunification, is following a policy mix that is eerily reminiscent of the Ronald Reagan–Paul Volcker mix, though for entirely different reasons. It's following a very expansionary fiscal policy and a very tight monetary policy. That's a big problem in Europe, where the hegemonic monetary power has parochial interests; so the Europeans are having problems. But in addition, Germany, with 7 percent (or whatever it is) of gross world product, is to some extent dragging the whole world along with its monetary policy—dragging the United States, which is several times its size, into an excessively tight monetary policy. I think that if we were reasonable, we wouldn't allow this to happen.

Cooper: So you would agree with Milton and Paul that monetary policy should be eased from where it is. Do you want to say by how much?

Krugman: 150 basis points.

Cooper: You're an interest-rate man. And now Milton.

Friedman: But, you know, I'm not in favor of fine-tuning.

Cooper: Give us some "gross-tuning." It has to be more than just the direction.

Friedman: I'm going to give you more than the direction, but I'm going to say that I'm one of those who believe very strongly that we ought to head to zero inflation and that we ought to adopt a monetary growth rate that will bring us to zero inflation in the long run. The problem I have with the monetary growth rate of the last three months is that it did have cyclical effects, so it was too low from a long-run point of view. I would like to see monetary growth increase enough to bring the average rate of growth on a secular basis to something like 4 to 5 percent, which is what I think we need to continue on the course of disinflation.

Cooper: This is on M1?

Friedman: No, no; not on M1.

Cooper: I'm just trying to be clear.

Friedman: The best measure from the inflation point of view is M2, which has a very high relationship with the long-term rate of inflation after a two-year lag. And it's on the basis of the past performance of M2 that I'm highly confident—differing in this way from Bob Mundell—that inflation is going to be coming down over the next couple of years; I won't predict beyond the next couple of years. But I think something like an M2 growth rate of 3 to 5 percent is what I want.

Now I want to say some other things. First, with respect to Bob's concerns about driving the dollar down, which I think are warranted concerns, it's absolutely baffling to me why the Federal Reserve and the Treasury have accumulated something like $60–80 billion of foreign exchange. They've been driving the dollar down. Don't let me exaggerate that. I believe that the market is a very big one; I don't know anything about the magnitude of the effects, but you can be sure that the direction of the effects on the dollar is down. So the first thing they might do is to sell those foreign currencies, which would have the effect of expanding the monetary base, not by buying government securities, but by selling foreign exchange for dollars.

On another matter, I want to make a comment about the capital-gains rate. I agree thoroughly—100 percent—with Bob Mundell that, for reasons of equity, capital gains should be indexed. I think it's a disgrace and a scandal that the capital-gains tax rate has been very much higher than the intended rate because of the failure to allow for indexing. But also—and Bob, I am sure, would agree with me on this—interest rates should be indexed.

Cooper: Indexed in the tax system?

Friedman: In the tax system. I'm also in favor of the government issuing purchasing-power securities.

Johnson: Let me just say that we have done exactly this in the United Kingdom.

Friedman: Yes, you have.

Johnson: As you know, we have introduced indexing of government bonds. The trouble is that when they become popular, that's a bad sign; it means that people are expecting inflation to rise.

Cooper: Do you want to elaborate and tell us a little more about the experience in the United Kingdom? It's now been about a decade.

Friedman: My impression is that the real rate of return on those has been relatively stable.

Johnson: Yes, it has varied between 3 and 4 percent. It has been more stable than the real return on securities with nominal interest rates, and it has taken away some of the risk from institutional investment. It has therefore fulfilled a social purpose.

Cooper: These are indexed to the consumer price index?

Johnson: Yes.

Cooper [to Friedman]: And your proposal would be to index to the consumer price index?

Friedman: I don't really care—I'll let the Treasury decide what index to use. I don't mind if it's indexed to the CPI; I don't mind if it's indexed to the GNP deflator; I don't mind if it's indexed to the consumption component of the deflator. Almost any indexing would be better than what we have now.

Samuelson: Mr. Chairman, your question about what should be the posture of monetary policy in the relatively short run in terms of the business-cycle situation has gotten lost in a shopping list of fundamental reforms that most of us who speak to them have had for a long time and that we trot out in season and out of season. So let me simply say—and I speak as an expert (Bob Solow says he's an expert on sex because he thinks about it all the time)—I'm an expert on capital gain; I think about it all the time. And I would like to have it indexed for equity. I would like the tax also to be collected at death, and I could outline a lot of other improvements. But as for using this as a meaningful tool in short-run stabilization, that's about as ridiculous as having public works projects—putting post offices on the drawing boards. You're three recessions into the future before the full effects of the spending are known. So, with your permission, I'd like to go back to your question.

Mundell: The question was about economic policy to be followed—not just monetary policy.

Samuelson: I want specifically to follow up on the monetary policy aspects. Of course, if we have lots of time, we can discuss everything. One of the problems for monetary policy at this juncture is that we have a variable Treasury interest-rate curve in terms of duration. The conventional wisdom is that the Fed, if it behaves in an active enough way, can pretty much get the short-term nominal interest rates that it wants. But the Treasury curve may steepen if, for example, people of prudence in the marketplace think the Fed is soft on inflation. We did a lot of econometric studies back in the 1960s, and we arrived at the conclusion that you can't do much by way of policy to induce changes in the yield curve, so we have to accept the way the cookie crumbles.

I think this matter needs to be reexamined. Indeed, I want to register my distrust of the findings of econometrics of an earlier decade. I don't even admire wholeheartedly the econometrics of last week, and so I'm not sure that we shouldn't be studying whether, say, by changes in the approach to open-market operations, some nudging down of long-term interest rates would be possible. I would not call it fine-tuning because it would be very gross at best. But what will help preserve the banking system that is in the course of going down the drain—and Las Vegas will bet you on how many hundreds of banks still haven't got the bad news—is, in part, lower long-term interest rates. What is important for the housing-starts market, for commercial shopping-mall ventures, and so forth is longer-term interest rates. But it's a very crude device to be using very, very low short-term interest rates in order to get a very weak effect, or even a perverse effect, on the longer end.

In any case, what's to be feared is not the "pushing on a string" that was a realistic phenomenon in the 1930s, when short-term interest rates were three-eighths of 1 percent. That isn't what I fear. What I fear is that we might be losing in an induced steepening of the Treasury yield curve. The situation is particularly complicated by the international aspects. And so the bind on the Federal Reserve—I would call its weakening effectiveness per unit of action—is from the still latent inflation problem that's in the minds of people in the marketplace and the international competition of interest rates, particularly from the Bank of Japan and the Bundesbank. If we add that the Federal Reserve chairman tells the market that he has no powers and that the market has all the powers, to the degree that there's anything to self-fulfilling prophecies, he will reap the harvest of those Delphic statements.

Cooper: Would you, Paul, agree that Bob Mundell's suggestion of a reduction in the capital-gains tax, assuming that it could be brought about, would have something of the same effect on asset values, and hence on the balance sheets of financial institutions, as a reduction in the long-term interest rate?

Samuelson: I think you would get a short-term induced increase in relative demand by foreigners and natives for venture capital. But I think we're talking about farthings rather than pounds as far as short-run effects are concerned.

Johnson: I have a question on the capital-gains tax while we're still on it. I was under the impression that the point of this proposal by President Bush was in fact to increase tax revenue in the short run. In other words, it was seen as a measure that would damp down the economy by reducing the deficit. That was surely the reason for putting forward a capital-gains tax cut—that so many people would realize capital gains that tax revenue would increase in the short run.

Samuelson: Every pill requires a sugar coating. And the sugar coating that is argued is that, without losing revenue, you can reduce tax rates (Arthur Laffer, thou shouldst be here now). But the case for reducing the tax on capital gains ought to be discussed on its merits—long-run merits.

Mundell: I'm very glad to hear Paul Samuelson say that he's for indexing the capital-gains tax. While I think the nominal tax rate on capital gains should be lower, I think indexing the tax is far more important. In the studies that have been undertaken, indexing the tax over the past couple of decades would be equivalent to something like lowering the nominal tax rate to about 5 percent. So while Paul and I are in agreement that indexing is a good idea, I am not in agreement with his conclusion that we're talking about farthings. I recommend indexing as a long-term structural reform, but it's an optimal time to have it, now that we are in a recession. So it is not a trivial thing at all; it's a plum dropped in our lap, which would have strong effects in the very near future in changing the whole level of asset prices, in helping the savings-and-loan position, and in getting us out of the current recession.

John Rutledge: I would like to comment on a matter raised earlier, the credit-crunch question, which is related to the capital-shortage issue that Bob Solomon raised. The vantage point that I want to bring to this is from the underbelly of the economy—from the board room, from the portfolio manager, from the folks out there trying to earn a living. This credit crunch, as Paul Samuelson described it—small businesses unable to obtain credit on normal terms, businesses that would have been approved for loans a year ago but not now—is very real. I have lived through two Chapter 11 situations this year from companies that on operating grounds had every reason to live, but were taken out because they couldn't obtain working-capital financing. Small-business financing declined last year more than real-estate financing, because a business loan is much easier to kill. If you're in the middle of a building project, it's a tough loan for a bank to stop, but a line of working capital is a phone call away from cancellation.

But the theme in all this that interests me is something Milton talked about earlier. He said there's a lot of similarity between the credit-crunch story and the 1930s. In particular, we've had a Fed that's trying to achieve a zero-inflation target. I would like to ask, Inflation of what? There's a vast discrepancy now between inflation measures of services and inflation measures of goods. The inflation rate for goods is essentially zero—zero to 1 percent last year. For a steel company I was working with two weeks ago, the price of its product last year was down 7 percent. And the key dollar event out there is a decline in the price level of fixed assets in the United States. We've had something like a $500 billion net worth loss in the U.S. in the last year due to declining real estate prices. And there's the declining net worth of banks; this brings out the examiners, the examiners shut down the banks, and small companies can't get money. I would argue that the economy has probably been more affected by those sorts of events than it has been by traditional flow events, such as the budget deficit. If you ask what monetary policy would make the economy stable right now, I don't think there's an answer in terms of the Fed funds rate; the answer is in terms of the financial integrity of the collateral base, of the fixed-asset base.

Randall Hinshaw: I would like to comment on a matter raised by Milton Friedman, Robert Mundell, and Paul Samuelson—namely, the ups and downs of the dollar. Unlike Paul Samuelson, for whom I have great respect, as a rule I tend to be unhappy when the dollar goes down and not to worry when it goes up. I have been particularly critical of central bank efforts to push the dollar down, because in my view those actions tend to raise the U.S. price level.

There are two ways to push the dollar down by central bank action. One is through outright inflation—through excessive monetary expansion, a method that, if carried out far enough, could push the dollar down to zero. The other way is through sterilized intervention. Some people argue that this would not affect the overall U.S. price level; the rise in the prices of internationally traded goods would be offset by a fall in the prices of domestic goods and services. I don't think this is true. I would argue that the prices of most domestic goods are sticky, so that what you are likely to have as a result of dollar depreciation in these circumstances is a higher overall price level, because the higher prices of international goods are not fully offset by a fall in the prices of domestic goods. What you are likely to end up with, it seems to me, is an overall rise in the U.S. price level accompanied by increased unemployment in the domestic goods industries—in other words, stagflation.

Krugman: This is an answer to Randall Hinshaw, among others. There's a bogeyman out there, which is the idea that one ought to talk down or push down the dollar just for the hell of it. That's not what we're talking about. The question is, Should an expansionary monetary policy to bring us out of this recession be held back? Should we be unwilling to do it because we are afraid of the consequences of the fall in the dollar that would probably be the result? Then you have to ask whether it's reasonable to be worried. I would say that the last five years have shown that fears that a declining currency leads quickly to domestic inflation have not been borne out at all by experience. I would say also that we should bear in mind that what we're really seeing in the world right now is not a weak dollar but a strong mark—a mark that is strong because of very specific German circumstances. The idea that the United States, which is three times the size of the German economy, should be inhibited by fear of a change in the exchange rate from following a monetary policy that on every other ground is appropriate is just very wrong. We really need a strongly expansionary monetary policy, and we should exercise some benign neglect of the exchange rate while we pursue it.

Solomon: I agree with most of what Paul just said. I'd like to add to it, though, on the question of monetary policy, which we were asked to comment on. A number of earlier speakers assumed that the Fed has been constrained by external considerations, particularly regarding the dollar, in making decisions about easing policy. I'm not sure we have any evidence to support that. I don't know of any, and I follow the Fed fairly closely. Everybody says—and I agree with them—that the Fed has been slow in easing, but I'm not sure that's the reason.

The second point I'd like to make is one that was made earlier by Paul Samuelson. He felt that, whatever the Fed does, long-term interest rates may not come down as much in relation to Fed action as in the past. I think that's an important point. I agree with it, and that ought to be part of our analysis.

Cooper: Bob Mundell, in speaking to this issue of U.S. policy, had a kind of throwaway line, and I'd like to bring it forward to make sure people either agree with it or say why they don't agree with it. If I understood him correctly, he said that in today's circumstances a tax reduction, apart from the capital-gains tax, can be ruled out as an instrument of policy. Implicit in this was that fiscal policy is hamstrung at the present time. Paul Krugman disagreed with that on the expenditure side. Is there general agreement either that the United States cannot or, even if it could, should not reduce taxes at this time—capital gains aside, on which we've had some discussion?

Samuelson: Well, let me mention one possibility, and that comes from Senator Moynihan. Senator Moynihan has proposed that some of the reduction in the overall deficit that is now in the present system is unjust and should be got rid of by lowering certain increments of the payroll tax. And the usual reaction—I must confess it's partly my reaction—is, Heavens, can't we keep the social-security system out of this? Because it's only what it is because nobody understands it. If it really comes on the table for discussion, we won't get a better approximation to the kind of Paul Douglas saving-investment relations that we want; we will get a long-term tax reduction by way of the payroll tax. But since you asked, I'll tell you. That is a possibility—that people could be persuaded that we haven't jeopardized the sacred budget compromise that we have behind us, and that we could just get some more employment opportunity through a reduction in payroll taxes.

Krugman: I find it amazing that we are one-quarter, maybe, into a real full-blown recession, with monetary policy not really having moved, and we're already declaring that monetary policy is ineffective and that we'd better find some other tool.

Cooper: I don't think we said that monetary policy is ineffective—only whether we were really ruling out fiscal policy because, for one reason or another, it was hamstrung. In raising the question, I didn't mean to suggest that monetary policy is ineffective.

Krugman: Well, actually, I think we've been seeing how hard it has been politically to start doing something about what is ultimately a fiscal policy that is too loose, not too tight. I think that the Fed has enormous power to turn this situation around, even if there's somewhat less bang for the buck for various reasons. The Fed has an unlimited supply of bucks. I don't see anything that needs to be done outside the Board of Governors at this point.

Friedman: Again, I have long been in favor of a tax cut of any kind, of any description, at any time, whenever you can get it.

Cooper: But you're against fine-tuning. So this is the wrong time to do it?

Friedman: No, it's not the wrong time; any time is fine. And I am fundamentally in favor of tax cuts at any time because I sharply disagree with Paul Krugman's view that higher spending is a good thing. I think that attempts to use fiscal policy for stabilization have been counterproductive on the average; they have often been destabilizing. Paul Samuelson mentioned one reason; you start a big public works program, and it takes so long to get the thing into effect that it comes in at the wrong time. But there are other reasons, such as the one that Bob Mundell cited about the effects on the capital market.

Fundamentally, I have been in favor of reducing taxes at any time for the purpose of holding down government spending, because I think government spending is mostly wasteful and does harm. But in the present circumstances—and here I go along with Paul Samuelson, surprisingly—I think that the social-security tax on payrolls is one of the worst taxes we have in the books. It's a very inequitable tax, and it's a tax that nobody in this room would be in favor of if it weren't for this crazy association with social security. There's nobody in this room who would believe that a desirable tax is a flat-rate tax on wages up to some maximum. And so, if the cycle gives you a good excuse to get rid of it, get rid of it.

Mundell: Well, I wouldn't want my silence here to be interpreted as implying that I believe that, apart from the tax on capital gains, all the other taxes in the system should be changed. For many years, I have believed that the corporate income tax is a very bad tax, but necessary. It would greatly increase the efficiency of the U.S. economy if that were lowered to, say, 25 percent. I'm not pushing this or proposing it as a recession measure now. That would be politically absolutely impossible for this year and probably for the next two or three years also.

Cooper: It seems to me that, with the arguable exception of 1974–75, this is the first recession since the 1930s in which we've had such fragile balance sheets in this country. But I think we should now turn our attention to the situation in Germany.

4.

Monetary Problems of German Unification

Introduced by Otmar Issing

Chairman Cooper: I've asked Otmar Issing to lead off this afternoon with an exposition of the German situation. I should explain that he is now on the Directorate of the Bundesbank, but he's been there for only three months, so he presumably still maintains some of his independence from the central bank that he had before his appointment.

Issing: You mean independence of view?

Cooper: Right.

Issing: German unification and its economic consequences—that's a long story. I think it's an interesting story, but of course I don't want to bore you. I will concentrate on the subjects that are connected with our discussion this morning on monetary policy.

First, let me talk about the monetary union in Germany, or better, let us say, the extension of the D-mark area to the eastern part of Germany. It was done on one day—July 1, 1990. From this day on, we had a boom in West Germany and a slump in the eastern part of Germany; industrial production there is half of what it was before unification, and it remains at this low level. The great uncertainty for this region is coming from the export side—exports to the former COMECON countries that were subsidized at a very overvalued exchange rate in terms of the Russian currency. That ended at the beginning of this month [January 1, 1991], but at the moment nobody knows how it will work out. In the short run, the alternatives are paying transfers to the unemployed or paying subsidies for the exports. I don't like the idea of export subsidies, because it's much more difficult to get rid of them.

Be this as it may, the transfer payments to eastern Germany have been very large. These come back via private consumption of western goods, and that means that our partners in the European Community take part in this process. German imports from France, Spain, and so on have risen dramatically.

German unification has led to an increased demand for capital, which in turn has led to a rise in interest rates. The rise in long-term interest rates was evident last spring, much before the government's demand for capital had risen. At that time, nothing much had happened thus far in the market; it was just expectations. And after its initial rise, the long-term interest rate has remained almost the same over the year. Then the huge public deficits emerged, but the long-term interest rate didn't rise further. So we have reached a kind of equilibrium level.

The fiscal deficit may amount to as much as 5 percent of gross domestic product in 1991, and it is accompanied by a somewhat restrictive monetary policy. Milton Friedman referred to two options for German policy, one of which was inflation. I believe we can exclude that as a policy. We decided at the Bundesbank to continue in 1991 our policy of monetary targeting, and I wouldn't have dared to come to this conference and sit beside Milton Friedman without that knowledge. Since July 1, 1990, we have had a common monetary policy for Germany. You will understand that we can't have different regional monetary policies, we can't have different regional interest rates. There are a lot of people who don't grasp this point.

This is a difficult position, of course, for eastern Germany. It was not easy to fix a monetary target for 1991, because in the course of currency unification, the monetary aggregate for eastern Germany has risen more than we had expected. We were not certain what the demand for money in the eastern part would be—what people would hold in their bank accounts and what they would spend for consumption. But it seems that we have a pattern comparable to that, let's say 20 years ago, in West Germany at the corresponding income level. So we now seem to have a quite stable situation. The monetary-growth aggregate, so far as we can still measure it, has gone down. At the beginning of July, the growth rate of M3 in eastern Germany was 15 percent, and in the former West Germany, 3 percent. At the end of 1990, the rate for eastern Germany had come down to 13 percent. So people in the eastern sector took their D-marks, bought long-term bonds and so on—what one could expect but couldn't be sure of.

How has German reunification affected the European Monetary System? I must say that there have been some strange reactions, but the increased German import demand resulting from unification came at just the right moment for some of our western partners. It was a kind of political fine-tuning that nobody had planned. There was recession in the United Kingdom, some weakening of the economy in Italy and (to a lesser degree) in France, so the increased German demand for imports was quite welcome. What was not so welcome was the rise in interest rates.

In Europe we are in a kind of preliminary stage of monetary union, declaring changes in nominal exchange rates to be tabu. Nominal exchange rates within the EMS have not changed in four years; January

1987 was the last time, when the Italian lira was devalued by a small amount. Since then there have been different price trends within the EMS, so that real exchange rates have changed, and if we add to this the rise in interest rates, it is clear that German unification has put a strain on the system of fixed nominal exchange rates. We can interpret the present situation as a test of whether this exchange arrangement comprises an optimum currency area. If it does, we don't need any adjustments in nominal exchange rates; we can get adjustment through changes in wages and prices. If, however, the exchange-rate arrangement breaks down, I would conclude that the area covered by the EMS is not, or is not yet, an optimum currency area.

What, then, are the prospects for the European Monetary System in the future? I must be cautious. I should admit to you that when the EMS was founded in 1979, I was among those who were quite sure that it couldn't last long. But it has lasted up to now. Capital movements are free, and the system still works; in fact, it has worked quite well. I think the main explanation for its success is that in the 1980s the priorities in all the EMS countries shifted to the priority of fighting inflation. There was no longer any Phillips illusion in Europe in the eighties, and as a result, countries followed the monetary policy of the Bundesbank. If there is still consensus in the future on this policy setting, the exchange arrangements will survive, and I think we might then move very quickly in the direction of monetary union. But first let us see how this period of testing turns out this year and next year. The outlook will depend on the policies in our partner countries.

Cooper: Could you say a little bit about the prognosis for the German financial situation? You said you thought that this year the budget deficit would be roughly 5 percent of gross domestic product. That mainly reflects, if I understand it correctly, the large transfers out of the federal budget into the new states, the eastern Länder. How long do you expect that to go on without some response in Bonn on fiscal policy—in particular, without a tax increase? Germany of course can borrow readily, but at least in the past, the German public has shown a marked discomfiture with a substantial rate of build-up of government debt. So I assume that at some point the government will worry about the deficit continuing on the present scale.

Issing: Let me first stress one point I forgot. Because of reunification, Germany is changing from being a high net lender—net exporter of capital—to being not necessarily a net capital importer, in view of its big current-account surplus, but a much smaller net lender. The current-account surplus has been going down very rapidly. Now with respect to your question, the government has decided that the deficit has to be brought down within four years.

Cooper: By 1995?

Issing: By 1994. Little progress can be expected this year. At lunch someone cited Machiavelli—that you must do the cruelties at the beginning—and that's also true if you have an election. So the government may have already missed the opportunity to cut expenditures for purposes not connected with unification. In the election campaign, the coalition parties didn't say, "Read my lips," but they did say, No tax increase for German unification. Well, now comes the Gulf War, and I don't know what the outcome will be, but I think we shall get some tax increases. Which tax increases, I don't know—perhaps on petroleum or something like that. Our fiscal problem is compounded by the fact that our states, the Länder, also have growing deficits. They haven't spent much for the process of unification; the deficits have arisen for other reasons. But we have a bad combination of deficits at almost all levels of government.

Friedman: What is your monetary growth rate?

Issing: It's 4 to 6 percent; it hasn't changed.

Cooper: Are you referring to the monetary base or M3?

Issing: M3.

Cooper: Do you still have a target on the monetary base?

Issing: No, no. It was given up three years ago because of the high percentage of currency in circulation. We introduced a new tax that brought a big increase of currency in circulation, because people wanted to evade the tax.

Cooper: Was this an increase in the value-added tax?

Issing: No, it was a deduction from interest payments.

Johnson: A withholding tax.

Issing: So we had a huge increase of currency in circulation, and for that reason the Bundesbank changed its target to M3.

Johnson: Mr. Chairman, I wonder if I could add something to this from the British point of view. So far, the EMS is absorbing the shock of German reunification much better than many people might have expected, and there is actually less talk now about the need for exchange-rate changes than there was three or six months ago. I think one reason is that we can see, first of all, that Germany was uniquely well placed to absorb this kind of shock, because she started off with a current-account surplus of 4 percent of gross domestic product. This may now be run down to almost zero because of the need to increase imports. The increase in imports helps to keep inflation down; it increases the supply of goods in relation to the demand, and at the same time, by the accounting identity, the gap between excess savings and investment has been closed by a big increase in investment in eastern Germany. I think the main worry is what is happening to wages in the eastern sector. There does seem to be a certain amount of competitive bidding going on by the pan-German unions. If that can be kept under control or can be offset by productivity improvements, I think we may get only a 1 or 2 percent increase in inflation in the former West Germany.

Now if Germany did inflate a little bit faster than, let us say, France or the Benelux countries—the other low-inflation countries—this would actually be quite beneficial to the system. It would mean a real appreciation of the mark without any need for exchange-rate changes that would offset the real depreciation owing to the low inflation in Germany, which made Germany, perhaps, rather uncomfortably competitive within the EMS through the 1980s. I think that if we did have to have a realignment—I wouldn't exclude it in spite of the outlook being so far, so good—it wouldn't by any means prove that we haven't got an optimum currency area; I think it would just show that the system still has a certain degree of flexibility. Realignments can only be fairly small—within a 3 to 5 percent range, the way the system now operates—and if it were necessary to have a once-for-all, perhaps final, realignment in the system in order to accommodate the aftereffects of the reunification shock, I don't think that would by any means undermine the system. It could be seen as a once-for-all operation in the way that reunification clearly is a once-for-all operation.

If I could just turn for a moment to the monetary consequences of what's happening in Germany, are we all suffering from having to have higher interest rates on account of what's happened to German interest rates? Within Britain, yes we are, but we intended that this should be so, because we have a policy of imposing recession on the economy in order to get our inflation rate down. And this is actually quite helpful; it means that there is no conflict now between our exchange-rate obligations as a new member of the EMS and our monetary policy, which has to be tough and requires high interest rates. So as far as we're concerned, this is quite a good development. We think that our currency is reasonably competitive with the D-mark, maybe not so much with the dollar, but you shouldn't believe everything you hear from those in the chemical industry, who are the main people going around saying that the pound is much too high. For many industries, the present rate of exchange is quite competitive. It's even rather low by purchasing-power-parity standards, but perhaps one shouldn't place too much reliance on those.

Now for the other member countries—maybe for France—their interest rates are a bit higher than they would like, but the remarkable thing is that France and Holland have actually been able to cut interest rates against German rates without any bad consequences for their exchange rates. And this, I think, is a very good example of how the system is able to adjust. We're no longer in a system where the D-mark is necessarily the strongest currency all the time. There is even a risk premium on D-marks against guilders; the guilder at certain times, at certain time horizons, appears to be the strongest currency in the system. So all rush and buy guilders; that's my tip! But I would say that this is really quite a comforting scenario for those of us who believe that monetary union is not only desirable but possible within, say, a decade—let's not be too ambitious. Perhaps in another part of this conference we might go a bit more deeply into monetary union itself and how that will operate, but I think from the point of view of Germany's partners, things are really going better than we might have hoped.

Krugman: Well, I don't think I want to argue the question of how well European monetary integration is proceeding so far. I think we need a little while. But I have found something to disagree with—the question of whether, if a realignment proves necessary, this shows that Europe is not an optimum currency area. The area is not being run as a true currency area, a true single-currency zone, would be. It's being run as if the Federal Reserve Bank of San Francisco were setting monetary policy for the whole United States but conditioning its policy only on California objectives: it's being run by a central bank that is ultimately answerable only to the national government of a single part of the whole. And that's not what would happen if you had a true European central bank.

Let me back up a bit. I think the explanation for the success of the exchange-rate mechanism of the EMS until now is that it rather fortuitously turned out that the system came into being just as fighting inflation became the supreme priority of all the nations of Europe. The great good fortune was that the largest economy in Europe also had the most determinedly disinflationary central bank, so everyone was prepared to hitch a ride on the Bundesbank's credibility and to forsake all the usual reasons why they might not be willing to accept hegemony by a single central bank. That meant that the system worked very well, because everyone was willing in effect to defer, even though the system was asymmetric. One might say that the D-mark area, in fact, was extended to all of Western Europe, contrary to what Christopher was implying.

Ultimately, that won't work well. There's bound to come a point at which a central bank that is, after all, only one country's central bank will find itself with objectives and interests that differ from those of the rest of the system. Let me go back to my analogy. Suppose that not only was the Federal Reserve Bank of San Francisco making policy for the whole of the United States and answering only to California, but there was also a boom confined to California, and the San Francisco Bank were to say, Our objective is to stabilize the price level of California, regardless of what deflation that might impose upon the rest of the country. That's not what a Federal Reserve System for the whole United States would do. Even if it was not as committed to price stability as you might like, it would attempt to maintain stability of the average price level across the country—not try to prevent any rise in prices within any single region, which would impart a deflationary bias to the whole economy.

So we actually have a very serious problem here. It's difficult to make out whether this is really going to be an issue, but the logic of it certainly suggests that what is going to happen is that, in the attempt to maintain stable prices in Germany, the Bundesbank is going to be tipping the rest of Europe into a recession. And I will continue to believe that that's what's going to happen until I see very strong evidence that it isn't. Let me put it this way. I don't think Europe did the homework; I don't think that the ground was properly laid for even this interim currency area. It has worked well by accident, by lucky accident, for ten years, and I think that people have been getting too complacent about it.

Mundell: I think one of the differences between us around this table comes from different views of the ease of adjustments to particular shocks in the system. We have this wonderful controlled experiment of what's taking place in Germany, the unification of Germany, and one of the questions is, What will be the impact of this additional German spending on world interest rates? Well, if Germany accounts for 7 percent of world GNP and if the German budget deficit accounts for 5 percent of German GNP, that deficit accounts for only about a third of 1 percent of the world demand for capital. It's hard for me to understand why that should have a really big impact on world interest rates. It should have some effect in an upward direction, but it is easy to exaggerate the extent of that effect.

The second question is, How inflationary will the budget deficit be inside Germany? My inclination there is to say, Not nearly as much as might be expected. Christopher Johnson made the point—and I agreed with most of what he said—that if the German trade surplus is reduced by 5 percent and the budget deficit is increased by 5 percent, that washes out, more or less. Now there will be other effects, there will be second-order effects, but there won't be any primary inflationary impact from that.

The third question is, What should be the effect on the D-mark exchange rate of the declining trade surplus that could disappear or even become a trade deficit? There's a difference in opinion about this, a difference that's been around for a long time, concerning the question of how easy or difficult it is for a transfer to take place and whether that requires a change in the exchange rate. It seems a little strange to me to hear that because Germany is now going to run a big budget deficit, it should suddenly need to appreciate the currency. The traditional argument would have gone in the other direction. The argument for appreciation, I think, comes from a model that says that a reduction in the German trade surplus is going to be inflationary because there will be more spending in Germany. Part of that spending will be on domestic goods and part of it on international goods, and the part that's spent on domestic goods will tend to raise the price level, whereas the part that's spent on international goods will not; so the overall effect will be to raise the price level. But I think this involves too pessimistic a view of the ease with which Germany can transfer resources from one direction to another—can shift resources into the construction trades and other areas as required. On the supply side, I am an elasticity optimist, and I don't believe that any change in the exchange rate is needed at all. I think that the necessary shifts can take place—especially in the situation that Germany is now in—at fairly constant cost. So I don't see an argument for appreciation.

Now there is a kind of argument as to why Germany might appreciate because of an increased budget deficit, going along on the old . . .

Frankel [interrupting]: Mundell-Fleming model [laughter].

Mundell: I was trying to paraphrase that [more laughter]. But that results from an increase in the demand for money, and the problem is easily solved by a more elastic monetary policy than would otherwise be necessary. I agree with everything that Christopher Johnson said about the extent to which any weakness or any slight expansionary policy in Germany, even if it's slightly inflationary, will come as a great blessing to France and to Italy, which already find Germany rather tight. If Germany wants to keep the European currency area without a basic realignment, then it just needs to have a slightly more expansionary monetary policy to make up for whatever increase in the demand for money there is, and this will not really involve a very substantial increase in overall inflation in Germany.

Samuelson: I have some genuine questions—one small question for Christopher and a number of more fundamental questions about the German situation. My desire is to learn more about the facts. First, my question to Christopher. If I were a member of the Federal Reserve System, like Lee Hoskins in Cleveland, who seems to be most interested in tackling and improving the inflation situation in America, then the logic that you were describing would be very welcome to me if what's happening in the United Kingdom would be what he might want to happen to the United States. The question I would put to you is this. We are told that Canada and Britain were in a recession—a National Bureau kind of recession—before the U.S. was in that situation. You have a new prime minister, you have elections ahead, but apparently the implicit possible increase in unemployment or continuation of higher than desired unemployment doesn't displease you. Do you just belong to a narrow banking economist club?

Johnson: No.

Samuelson: Or is there a wide constituency in your country that shares your way of appraising good and bad events?

Johnson: Well, let's say, if the German shock hadn't happened, we might be in the position of needing to lower interest rates sooner than we wanted to on domestic grounds in order to prevent the pound from appreciating against the D-mark, which was the danger that people feared before we entered the EMS. As it turned out, this was 180 degrees wrong; we have had to keep our interest rates higher for longer than we wished, although we have begun to cut them. I think the general view is that if we're going to have to take some unpleasant medicine, let us take it in one dose; let's get the agony over instead of having to do it again after an election. And as inflation comes down, which it will in Britain this year, we shall be able to lower our nominal interest rates, while keeping real interest rates still rather high—and perhaps higher than they will be in Germany. So I think it does just about work out; it's quite a narrow tightrope, but we haven't fallen off it yet.

Samuelson: All right, well, now to the German situation. I would like Otmar Issing's guesses as to how things are likely to work out in real terms, policy aside. By and large, *perestroika* everywhere in Eastern Europe has up to this point been a great disappointment. Things get worse before they get better, and the disappointments certainly are very far from having all been registered. Eastern Germany in a sense is a controlled economy that is specially favored in its move toward a market economy. Before the unification, our best estimators of the real GNP per capita in East Germany said—and I think they were off the beam—that it was about 80 percent of the West German level. The second thought of most people who are not quite as expert is that maybe something like 50 percent would have been a more realistic figure for the ante-unification situation.

So I want to ask Otmar this, What is the relative position from which East German real per capita production and productivity start, at what pace is the huge differential with West Germany being wiped out, and what is the presumed asymptote that is ahead in the middle 1990s? Not a very simple question to put to you, but any guesses that you can give would be extremely useful, because one can't really judge complex policy questions unless one knows what the general landscape is likely to be.

Issing: The question is, How long does it take to get a comparable capital-labor ratio in eastern Germany? We start out from a position that in recent months has been getting worse, though perhaps we have now reached bottom. But the estimates for eastern Germany as compared with the former West Germany are really below 50 percent. I won't say more, because that would only be guessing. But the wage increases in eastern Germany are very, very high. The background for this is of course the movement of labor within one country with the same language; that's very easy. At the moment, the only reason why we don't have more emigration from east to west is because of the housing problem in the west and the very low rents in eastern Germany; that makes the real-wage differential much lower. But the process is complicated because before unification wages in the east had almost no differentiation, and so in order to keep the very active and highly qualified workers there and also in order to attract people from the outside—we need migration from the west to the east—it is necessary, of course, to pay them salaries at the western level. That causes big differences in wages. Within a bank or within an office, there may be somebody earning a western salary while next to him, doing the same work, is somebody earning only a third or a fourth as much.

In this situation it's almost unavoidable for wages to rise much more rapidly than productivity, and that means that unemployment may be a serious problem. It also means large-scale transfer payments from west to east. So Germany for a time, I think, will be quite absorbed with the problems of unification. But we are, after all, a small country, and our impact on interest rates in the world is not big, though from a European perspective, I think, it still matters.

Cooper: My question to Otmar is concerned with the question of inflation and targeting the price level. More particularly, I would like to know exactly what price level you are targeting, as it concerns the adjustment mechanism that Bob Mundell referred to. You have the same problem in measuring the price level that you alluded to in measuring the money supply, because you take two geographic areas and combine them. You have a statistical service in the old Federal Republic; you now have the problem of integrating into a national index the eastern Länder—the five new Länder—and their prices. The structure of their prices, as I understand it, is internationally integrated now since unification. Tradable goods carry the same prices, approximately, because they can move freely, but nontradables—mostly services—have much lower prices, measured in D-marks. That would be especially true of rents, but it would also be true of physician services, for example, and other services that are geographically confined. What that means is that in any national index, as those prices rise to West German levels, the overall German price level goes up unless there are compensating price reductions in West Germany. If the West German price level is prevented from falling and is kept stable, the overall German price level will rise, and that will be seen by anyone who looks at the index as inflation. It will not be felt by West Germans as inflation, but of course it will be felt by East Germans as inflation.

So the question is, When the Bundesbank targets the price level, is it or is it not making allowance for this very special factor? This is important because it raises the question of the adjustment mechanism. If the main source of fiscal stimulus in Germany for now and the immediate future is, in fact, transfer payments, and the transfers are spent mostly on tradable goods, those tradable goods, as you pointed out, can come from all over Europe—indeed, from all over the world—not just from the former West Germany. There is no reason why there should be any significant inflation from that source, apart from the little adjustments in margins that take place. But there will be an inflationary impetus stemming from nontradable goods as transfer payments replace subsidies in eastern Germany. And if you are targeting the new national price level, it seems to me that you actually impede the adjustment process. This issue is somewhat technical but, I think, potentially important, so I am asking whether you are going to allow the adjustment mechanism to work, in which case you do get some relative price changes but mostly in nontradable services, or are you going to impede that process from working?

Krugman: I just want to register the idea that there are not two rigid classes of tradables and nontradables.

Cooper: No, of course not.

Krugman: Distance is a key factor; things that might be tradable across 50 kilometers may not be tradable at 500 kilometers. And, in fact, many of the things that may be reasonably considered to be tradable between the new and the old Länder of Germany may not be tradable as far as France or the United Kingdom. That's a very important point.

Friedman: You can drive twenty miles to get a haircut.

Krugman: Yes. And you may ship cement a little bit further than where you go to buy a haircut, and you may be able to ship perishable produce a certain bit further. Other items may stop at the customs frontier. Analytical simplification is very useful for some purposes, but it may be quite misleading here.

Issing: Let me begin my answer to Richard Cooper's question by saying that when we were engaged in monetary targeting for the new Germany, we took into account that the eastern part is only 10 percent of the whole. That helped us a lot.

Samuelson: Instead of 17 percent? You call it only 10 percent?

Issing: Yes, with respect to the production potential, it's about 10 percent, and now it seems to be still less. For population the situation is different, but for production it's 10 percent or less. And we thought about the price index in the same way. Thus far, there is no national price index, and I think for the near future there shouldn't be one, because, you see, people buy such different goods in the east and the west and have such different incomes. I think it makes no sense now to put it together. But the problem still exists, of course, and what has happened, to the surprise of many, is that prices in the east for nontradables actually fell.

Cooper: Fell?

Issing: Fell; they didn't rise. We had expected that there would be big price increases, but this didn't happen; prices expressed in D-marks fell. Rents in eastern Germany are negligible; the tenants pay almost nothing. As for heating, the problem of controlling the temperature was always solved in the past by opening or closing the window. And nothing has happened so far. It has just been announced that the price for rent, including heat, will be doubled from one D-mark to two D-marks, but the increase is only a compensation for the cost of heating.

This means that in the future there must be huge price increases, but that would not be inflation in any sense that should be assigned to monetary policy. So I think that for a while we should stay with the West German price level for a monetary target.

Friedman: My comment goes back to this distinction between recorded figures and real figures. You mentioned earlier that production in eastern Germany had gone down by 50 percent. I don't believe it. Production went up. You had people producing negative products, and now at least they're moving toward zero products.

Issing: They're still useless products.

Friedman: Oh, yes, they're still useless. You still have further to go in this direction, but after all, if people are wasting resources, it's better to pay them to stay at home and do nothing. I am reminded of an old example of this that is really very relevant. In the reforms that were taking place in Chile back in the early 1970s when they were trying to cut down government spending, to eliminate wasteful spending, but they had contracts to pay civil servants, they told them to stay home— that the civil servants would get their pay but were not to come to the office, because if they did, they would be using precious resources.

Now this observation applies to a remark that Paul Samuelson made. He said that *perestroika* had been a real disappointment in the Eastern European countries. I can't speak for all of them, but Rose and I spent some time in Poland in September, and the recorded figures in Poland show an incredible drop in production. But that's a fake; it's an utter fake because there is a big nonrecorded market. Whether it's a black market or a legal market, God only knows, but nobody's trying to stop it. There's an informal market in which performance has been really rather good and in which there has been a substantial increase in output.

Moreover, there are a lot of people in Poland who are going as tourists to Germany and Britain and so on and working there illegally. The estimates we heard of how much capital they are bringing back to Poland were really astonishing. So there is a real inflow of capital into Poland that's coming in this indirect way, by people going out, working, and bringing money back. And although the official figures for Poland were that output in September, when we were there, was down very sharply from the year before, those people who are close to the informal market and to the other developments in Poland argued that this just wasn't so—but in the real standard of life, the real goods available. There were some sharp increases in quality, and there was a very great difference between some people and other people, but taken as a whole, the official figures were grossly understated as applied to production.

The next comment I want to make is of a very different kind. Paul Krugman raised the question this morning of how the world works. As I've been listening to him, to Christopher, to Bob Mundell, and to Paul Samuelson, we are all working on exactly the same assumptions; there isn't any fundamental difference in our theoretical views. But what's striking is how wide the differences are in our empirical predictions. I think, for example, that the EMS is going to be subject to very severe strains in this next year or so, and I expect it will break down. It may not break down, but there will be some significant revaluations there, and that will postpone any hope of having a single currency for Europe. Christopher is much more optimistic on that score. So, I gather, is Bob Mundell. The point is that differences in empirical predictions do not necessarily require differences in views of the way the world works.

Cooper: Let me ask a specific concrete question, because it has been implicit in a number of the remarks—that the impact of what's happened in Germany, given unchanged exchange rates, is going to be contractionary. I would like first to put that on the table explicitly and, secondly, raise the question of whether it's true. You have an injection of spending in Germany which is new, which wasn't there before, and that injection, in my view and in Bob Mundell's certainly, is going to spill throughout the Community, not to mention the rest of the world. On the other hand, because the injection of spending is being financed—let us say entirely, for the sake of argument—by going to the capital market, there is upward pressure on interest rates, and the effect of that on aggregate spending is negative. We have two factors pushing in opposite directions. The question is—and this puts to a test Milton's proposition that we all have the same model—Do we share a view on the net effect of these opposing factors? My view—and here I am a little puzzled by what Christopher said—is that the net effect on aggregate demand is going to be positive, not negative.

Krugman: But the question has to be, What do we think the Bundesbank is going to do?

Cooper: That's a different question. I'm assuming for the sake of this argument that the Bundesbank has its monetary target and is not going to deviate from it.

Johnson: Well, can I say that the answer obviously depends on two things. One is a country's share of the German import market—our share is much less than that of France, for example—and the other is how far one's currency tends to be influenced by the D-mark in world markets. Having more of a world currency than the French, we are rather more at the mercy of German interest-rate influence.

Cooper: Fair enough; so the answer could differ for different countries. But what I was trying to test was Milton's proposition that we share a model, and one way of testing it is on this quantitative point.

Friedman: We share the model; we differ on the parameters. You're assuming different elasticities than I'm assuming.

Cooper: And that's often critical for policy choices and for predictions.

Friedman: You're absolutely right; that's my whole point.

Samuelson: All my life, Milton has been telling me that I share the same model that he does [loud laughter].

Friedman: You do!

Samuelson: There's a person [Milton Friedman] who is six inches from me, and I consider myself six feet from him—that's peculiar Euclidean geometry. The reason why I think differences in models—as between, say, Paul Krugman and Robert Lucas—make a big difference is the following. If I weren't as near to Krugman as I am, and was a lot nearer to Bob Lucas than I am, I would think the adjustments imposed on countries as part of a pegged currency arrangement would be quite easy to make in real welfare terms that I'm concerned with, and I might well go down the sawdust trail to be with Randall Hinshaw toward more stable exchange rates. But I don't believe that the mechanisms work in that way. And therefore Milton and I, when we agree on our policy recommendations, do so for different reasons. He has a different model than I have in quantitative respects, and he also has different ethical ends. And I just hope this goes on for another 40 years [more loud laughter].

Mundell: Well, I think it would be interesting to put these questions about the big changes that are going on in Europe into a different framework. Suppose we transpose the situation to the United States, where there have been great regional shifts. If we go back to 1985, for instance, the sharp fall in the price of oil really devastated the economy of Texas and much of the southwest. Then, assuming a system of fixed exchange rates with separate currencies within the United States, Milton would have said that it was impossible to make the adjustment without a devaluation of the Texan dollar. And by the same token, he might want to say that with the recent increase in the price of oil that has wreaked havoc in the New England economy, an appreciation of the New England dollar would be desirable. But I don't believe that at all, not because the drop in real income in the two regions isn't serious, but because the exchange-rate changes wouldn't be of any help in improving those situations. A big devaluation wouldn't make the problem in Texas one iota easier. Texas would end up with a legacy of a 20 or 30 percent higher price level than the rest of the country, with all the effects that this would set in motion.

Transposing that now to the real world in Europe, it's true that countries are going to have some difficult regional problems if they move toward a common European currency, and there will have to be a centralized policy that will involve certain regional problems, but I don't believe that exchange-rate changes were ever any good in solving those problems. In practice, that's the difference between the models that we have. Milton has the view that changing the exchange rate and therefore the value of debts and the real value of wages, combined with money illusion, can work. I accept the fact that his argument for flexible exchange rates is based upon money illusion and that he believes in money illusion. I don't believe in money illusion in that sense. Whatever benefits you get in the short run, you always pay for later on.

Friedman: There are two very separate issues involved in what Bob is saying. One is the issue of whether if Texas, New England, and so on had separate monetary systems with pegged exchange rates between them, they would have changed their exchange rates. The second issue is whether it would have done any good. With respect to the first issue, I have no doubt whatsoever that if, indeed, Texas had an independent monetary system and its own independent separate central bank, it would have had a devaluation. And I have no doubt at all that New England would have altered its exchange rate. But I believe there's an absolutely fundamental difference between a unified currency and a set of national currencies held together by pegged exchange rates.

And that's the same with Europe. If Europe really had a common currency, or if it were back on a pure gold standard, or if somehow all the central banks in Europe disappeared except the Bundesbank, I accept Bob's argument completely that the European countries would adjust to it, as they did in the nineteenth century when the situation was like that. But that isn't the situation. The situation in fact is that all of these countries have separate central banks, and they are not going to be willing to behave as they would behave if they had a unified currency instead of a set of national currencies.

Now the next question is, Would changing the exchange rate do them any good or not? And Bob may well be right; in the long run, it would do them no good. But it would do them good in the short run. In this respect, like Paul Samuelson, I am not very close to the extreme view of Bob Lucas and others on rational expectations. I believe there is money illusion in the short run. I think it's a very real thing in the short run, though it isn't rational in the long run. But in the short run I think it would help the transition. Maybe it would be a mistake; I'm not saying it wouldn't be. I'm only making an empirical prediction that if we have these separate central banks, they will not in fact be willing to act as if they had a unified currency.

Mundell: I would like to say that the harmful effect doesn't just depend upon the money illusion argument. It depends also upon the fact that if Texas did devalue, then the next time the problem happened, the same remedy would be expected again, which would set in train a whole series of events. So central bank credibility is extremely important. Otmar Issing's boss, Governor Poehl, once said that credibility is the capital stock of every central bank. So past history builds up expectations, and the Bundesbank has credibility because it has a great track record of 30 years.

I don't completely agree with Milton's statement, because I think that you can have a credible system of fixed exchange rates with national currencies if central banks operate in the forward exchange market to fix forward rates. That drives interest rates down, and you can duplicate the benefits of a common currency with a system of separate currencies and fixed exchange rates. In the real world, what we're talking about is not the system we now have in Europe but a new system in which two alternative approaches are being considered. And when we talk about the best way of creating a European currency, I think that Milton's argument will come up, because the question is whether to create a unified currency like the dollar in the United States or to create a kind of fixed exchange-rate zone in Europe. I think Milton's arguments are quite relevant here. If it turns on that issue, the big issue—an ecu kind of system or a unified currency system—I opt for Milton's solution, the unified currency system.

Willett: Two quick points. The first is with regard to the analogy between a potential European currency and the U.S. currency area. Barry Eichengreen has pointed out that there is a very strong fiscal cushioning mechanism in the United States, so that a very substantial part of the shock in Texas, for example, was offset through fiscal transfers. Secondly, on the issue of the effectiveness of exchange-rate adjustments, I think it's important to recognize that we don't have to rely on money illusion. There can be serious frictions in collective decision-making when you have multiple rational actions, which can make it much more difficult to bring real-wage declines than when the real-wage decline is achieved, not by cutting nominal wages, but by holding nominal wages constant and permitting the price level to rise. So the argument for exchange-rate adjustments to have an effect is reinforced by money illusion, but doesn't have to rely on it.

Samuelson: Hear, hear.

Frankel: I assume that the term *money illusion* is being used in a broader sense to mean something having real implications. We did seem for a moment to have one of those fundamental differences of view as to how the world works when Bob Mundell elucidated what's called in the pages of the *Wall Street Journal* the Mundell-Laffer hypothesis—that a nominal devaluation is very rapidly passed through into prices and has no real effect. But then I was pleased to hear Milton Friedman speak on the other side of that one, at least in the short run. Paul Krugman mentioned early on that the experience of the 1980s— the very high correlation between nominal exchange rates and real exchange rates—seemed to supply a piece of evidence in favor of the view that there is money illusion and that nominal exchange-rate changes have real effects.

I'd like to bring up another possible piece of evidence, although it's an open question, and it brings us back to the subject of German monetary union. Last year, when it first appeared likely that East Germany and West Germany were going to unite, there was some debate as to what the exchange rate for the two German currencies should be. Figures suggested that the productivity rate in East Germany was maybe a third, at best, of that in West Germany, and there was some discussion that if there was unification, the terms of exchange could not be one for one—one East German mark for one D-mark. Two for one, perhaps, or three for one, but surely not one for one. Yet that's what happened. Now many of my fellow American economists with whom I have discussed this say it doesn't matter; wages and prices can adjust freely, and it's purely a nominal issue at what rate you peg. My impression is that it would matter—that wages in eastern Germany would not costlessly and evenly fall to reflect the true levels of productivity, that nobody would want to build a new factory with the lower productivity level, and that parity for the two currencies would be a mistake that would hold back eastern Germany. And my understanding is that wages have not adjusted in the correct direction.

Cooper: They've gone up rather than down.

Frankel: Yes, and I think the reason is that the transition to a market system is a difficult one. Every person, every individual worker, has to discover for himself or herself that they're in a different world—that if they can't produce what's wanted, they're going to be out of a job. And it is a difficult psychological adjustment to make. I think a valuable opportunity to demonstrate this lesson was lost. The lesson that I think a typical East German worker learned in this episode is that the way you attain the standard of living they have in West Germany is through politics, not through economics—that going on strike or voting for Kohl is the way you attain a western living standard. And that's a lesson that sooner or later is going to have to be unlearned.

Issing: I fully agree. There should have been a transitional period to permit adjustments to take place smoothly. There should have been an exchange rate of, say, two to one, or something like that. Matters were made worse because people in eastern Germany expected prices to rise, so the unions said, We must have compensation—and they got it. But when the figures came out, the price level in East Germany had actually fallen. So that made matters even worse.

But let me make a comment on Paul Krugman's comparison of the Federal Reserve Bank of San Francisco with the Bundesbank's position in Europe. I would like to make two points. The first is that when we speak of European unification, we mean that the future monetary policy of Europe will be pursued in the manner of the Bundesbank, but without the Bundesbank—and of course not just for Germany but for the European Monetary Union as a whole. The second point is with respect to regional shocks. I think we all agree that in an optimum currency area you must have either a high degree of mobility of labor or a system of transfer payments. Up to now, neither of those requirements exist in Europe, and I'm not at all sure that Europe is yet in a situation where financial transfers would be paid willingly by one country to another. Believe me, the transfer situation is already a source of great strain within Germany. There's a very bad joke that former East German Chairman Honecker received a prize, an award, from the West, and guess why—because he concealed the problem of unification for so many years! That's a bad joke, but it reflects the thinking of not a few people.

Solomon: May I contribute another joke?

Cooper: Yes, it's your turn.

Solomon: The one I heard is that the unification problem is rather easy, because, from the point of view of the West, it's like remarrying your former wife [laughter].

Issing: But she's grown older [more laughter].

Solomon: Very good. The less frivolous point I wanted to make is that there *are* differences around the table on how the world works. We have identified one here. Some of us believe that changes in nominal exchange rates have real effects or can have real effects, and at least one of us doesn't.

Mundell: Who's that?

Solomon: You, if I heard you correctly.

Mundell: But I've never said that; I've never said they have no real effects. That would be like saying that if you increase the quantity of money by 50 percent, it wouldn't have any real effects. Of course, ultimately there is a new equilibrium that in real terms may be similar, but in the transition process there are always real effects except in a world in which there were no rigidities, no money illusion, and no fixed debt. In any case, if a country were to double or triple its money supply, it would gain no new real resources from that action.

Frankel: Didn't you say earlier that you don't believe in money illusion?

Mundell: What I meant was that I don't believe in money illusion in the long run. For example, it doesn't do any good to say, Well, we have a recession looming, and all we need to do to get out of our difficulties is to pump more money into the system; that will establish full employment, and we'll all be better off. What I am saying is that this kind of policy after a certain point becomes useless because we would move into a classical type of world where everything becomes anticipated and money illusion disappears. The same applies to exchange-rate changes; the more a country relies on changes in exchange rates, the less useful they become.

Frankel: So we have the same model after all.

Krugman: Two points. First, if we all have the same model, we're disagreeing about parameters. In particular, we don't agree on how much money illusion there is—money illusion meaning how much price stickiness there is in the short run. We can say with much assurance that there is a great deal of price stickiness in the short run on the basis of what's been happening with exchange rates. We can also say that elasticities are not very high in the short run—that there are not, in the short run, massive shifts or substitutions of production on the basis of real exchange-rate differentials of 10 or 15 percent.

Mundell: What's your definition of the short run? Two days? Two years?

Krugman: Three years; I'm willing to settle for three years.

Mundell: Two decades?

Krugman: Three years; we don't have enough evidence for two decades. Second point: Otmar Issing's definition of what constitutes an optimum currency area definitely is not satisfied by the United States. If he is saying that an optimum currency area is one where there is sufficient factor mobility to enable the area to deal with regional shocks without the necessity for large changes in prices or sustained periods of unemployment within the adversely affected regions, the United States just doesn't meet that criterion at all.

Johnson: I would like to make the point that it's very difficult to generalize about how effective a nominal devaluation can be in creating a real devaluation, because it seems to me to depend on the extent to which the countries concerned do their trade with each other. In Western Europe we are doing an increasing proportion of our trade with each other; it's 50 percent for the United Kingdom; for several other countries in the EMS it's even higher. This means that nominal devaluations very quickly become ineffective because they are reflected in the price of imported products, which form an increasing proportion of expenditure. I think this is why talk about wishing to retain the devaluation weapon and not get too involved in economic and monetary union is beginning to have a certain dated look about it, particularly when one considers that we have the 1992 program which aims toward our doing an even higher proportion of our trade with each other, by bringing down the trade barriers.

So in this case I think it's certainly true that devaluation is a wasting asset. But in the case of the United States, which only does about 10 percent of its GNP in external trade, one can see that the devaluation of the dollar in the last few years has had an absolutely electrifying effect on manufactured exports. Sorry, that's not a bad pun; I didn't just mean the electrical industries. Dollar depreciation clearly has had an effect on all manufactured exports without in fact causing more than a sort of pimple on the consumer price index. I'm sure Paul Krugman will tell us that import prices don't respond immediately to exchange-rate changes, although perhaps by now they have, because the lower dollar is regarded as being permanent and not just a temporary fluctuation. But I stand ready to be corrected by our American experts on that.

Krugman: I'm puzzled by why you should focus on the share of trade that is conducted with other European countries. If there should be a devaluation of the pound, surely that would tend to raise the price of all imported goods.

Johnson: Yes, that's exactly my point.

Krugman: But then the right number surely is not the share of the United Kingdom's expenditure that takes place with Europe, but the share of U.K. expenditure that is imported, which is something under 30 percent—not much different from what it has been since the days of Queen Victoria. I don't think there's any particular reason to think that the rules of the game have been changed.

Johnson: Well, I think my hypothesis is that the price of imported goods is more likely to change if they're imported from Europe than if they're imported from other areas. But I may be wrong.

Rutledge: I think that the relative-price effects going on right now are very profound and very exciting. If you're talking about models, you should look at this business of a one-time very large bump in the risk-adjusted after-tax return on new capital goods in a sizable portion of the world—partly disguised by the fact that there is an economy in place for which there are no numbers. You have book values, you have government reports, and so forth, but the actual economic value being created isn't known. But there's this kernel of a new economy starting, and it seems to me that the appropriate model to look at is, say, postwar Japan or the United States in the 1800s or other episodes when there has been a new world—where there's a gap between risk-adjusted real returns on capital large enough to excite investors, large enough to cause other price effects to happen, and lasting long enough to encourage resources to flow.

For example, in the German case you had this show up in part as higher real interest rates, but you also had a rising stock market, which I think is very interesting. The portfolio manager who runs Fidelity's Equity Fund moved from the United States to London in October. He moved to London because, in his view and in Fidelity's view, the abnormally high real rates of return are now in Europe; they're not in the United States. So their best talent goes to Europe. Since last fall, the president of Lazard Frères investment firm has been in Germany 40 percent of the time. They're all playing the long side.

Cooper: Do you want to spend one minute on belaboring what may be obvious to everyone else except me? Why is the real rate of return on capital higher now in Europe than it was last year or two years ago?

Rutledge: Because eight months ago, if you had put new capital into East Germany, it would have been taken away from you. Very simply, there is now actually an opportunity to own the means of production in a place where before there was a wall between rates of return—where there were vast gaps between capital-labor ratios but no way for the market to exploit them. Now a market is gradually forming. It's the little one that Milton is talking about. It's not in the figures; you have to go there and talk with people to see it. I know of two dozen firms that are in projects to build enterprises in Eastern Europe that rely on bringing in new capital to take advantage of the low capital-labor ratio. The low capital-labor ratio has got to mean an abnormally high real return on capital and abnormally low real wages. And it's rational for workers in an enterprise that's going to die in a year to look for walking money; the more wages you get, the more money you have to go to Frankfurt with. That's what Otmar was talking about. We've seen tremendous flows of labor to the west and of capital to the east, which have the effect of reducing the gap between real rates of return. That's the gap I'm really talking about; it's the gap created by these resource imbalances.

Samuelson: Are you saying that a tremendous amount of productive labor that previously was imprisoned in the command economies of Eastern Europe is now available to be combined with the mobile capital goods of the west and that these mobile capital goods of the west are beating a path to the door there? Because much of what we hear, including much of what I heard here today, is sort of the reverse of that. The efficiency units that you as an employer get for the wages you pay sound to me very discouraging. If I were a footloose capitalist, I would entice workers to come to West Germany in order to become part of that system, rather than moving my capital out. You're nodding your head, but what's your answer to my question?

Rutledge: The answer to the first part is yes, and the answer to the second part is that I wouldn't buy an existing plant in former East Germany either. What I would want to do is to start from the ground up, and I think that this is where these small pockets of capital goods are going; they're going into small businesses and start-up operations where there is a high marginal product of capital. The efficiency of capital is higher now than it was a year go, which ought to show up in its price—in the same way that it did in Japan.

Cooper: In Japan you had a highly skilled labor force with a wage appropriate to its skill, and then through the war, the capital stock was destroyed. So you had a social structure with one factor missing. By replacing that capital stock, you got a big payoff. Let's distinguish East Germany from the rest of Europe, because the two areas are quite different in my view. In the case of East Germany, you have people who, let us say (for that's a question), were being paid the appropriate wage, given their system. Then you change the system, and you pay them a higher wage, but their training hasn't improved, their productivity hasn't improved at all. I'm having trouble reconciling that with a big jump in the marginal productivity of capital as seen from a global point of view. Poland is a somewhat different case. If you believe the figures (although Milton, I think rightly, has cast doubt on all the official figures), there has been a decline in real wages. And there you might well imagine that if people find the new system credible, the return to capital will go up. So far there has not been a great rush of western capital into Poland; there are examples here and there, but there hasn't been a great rush. People are waiting to see whether the marginal return to capital is in fact going to be higher for the relevant horizon for these investments. But in East Germany I would have thought not.

Issing: Perhaps you got too pessimistic an impression from my remarks. There are really many investment opportunities in the eastern part of Germany. In the short run, investment has been slowed by the wage increase, but from all that we have learned from managers, the labor force is doing quite well. And in certain respects, East Germany has had important advantages not shared by the rest of Eastern Europe. The replacement of its currency with the D-mark meant that, at the same moment, eastern Germany imported the price system of the west. The German legal system was also extended eastward, so that eastern Germany didn't have to go through the long process of building institutions.

In the banking industry, productivity is growing very rapidly because management from the west is coming in. And at every level of industry, eastern Germany is importing human resources and know-how. Public servants from the west come for half a year or so, and the Bundesbank has brought all its knowledge there. So it's a mixed process, and I overstressed a bit, perhaps, the pessimistic side of the picture. But the service section, which isn't included in the recorded decline of industrial production, has been growing very, very rapidly. The statistics there are always lagging behind, because it's small business mostly.

So, overall, I'm quite optimistic. I think what has happened in eastern Germany will be regarded as a success story if the politicians don't make too many mistakes.

5.

International Policy Coordination Reconsidered

Introduced by Jeffrey A. Frankel

Chairman Cooper: Let me take stock briefly. We've talked now about the U.S. situation without resolving it, although I think there was a general consensus that a decline in interest rates would be desirable in the immediate future. We've talked at some length about Germany, also without resolving matters, but I take it there's general assent that German interest rates are going to stay high, given the likely large budget deficit. So we have two very important economies whose developments we have discussed. Curiously enough, we have hardly discussed Japan at all, which is interesting because it seems to me that Japan was almost the only country we talked about at our last meeting.

The question I'd like to propose now is what implications, if any, these diverse developments have for policy coordination among countries. Jeff Frankel has been working a lot on policy coordination, not as to whether it's a good thing or a bad thing, but just as a thing that deserves study. So I've asked him to make a few remarks on what lessons, if any, he thinks the current configuration has for policy coordination and what the Group of Seven should be doing. What should it have done last weekend, for example, and what should it be doing over the next year or so?

Frankel: I'm going to make a little pitch for nominal GNP targeting, which won't surprise anybody who read my little paper that was circulated ahead of time and which applies to international policy coordination within G-7 meetings as well as to national policy making. One of the first questions we talked about this morning was whether the United States should be expanding a bit on monetary policy now to resist the recession. How should that be phrased? Paul Krugman phrased it in terms of a fall in interest rates. Milton Friedman phrased it in terms of a rise in the money-growth rate. What the correct target should be for the United States and, I would say also, for Europe is still a very open issue. We have been talking about whether Europe is an optimum currency area and whether exchange rates should be fixed between Germany and other countries, but accepting for now the idea of fixed exchange rates, there is still a question about Europe in the aggregate. What should be the nominal target for European expansion?

I think that we could get a broad consensus that some degree of commitment to a credible target, a nominal target of some sort, is desirable. Not an absolute commitment—maybe Milton would like a stronger commitment than some of the rest of us, but nobody wants an absolute commitment. And nobody wants complete discretion. Discretion on a year-to-year basis often results in a greater degree of inflation than we want. There was a consensus at the end of the 1970s that we needed some degree of commitment to a nominal target. The big victor then was Milton Friedman and monetarism, and there was some degree of commitment to M1 as we moved into the 1980s. The commitment to M1 was abandoned implicitly by Paul Volcker in the second half of 1982. I can remember in 1981, when I was working at the Council of Economic Advisers, going to meetings where Beryl Sprinkel would lecture representatives from the Fed that M1 had broken outside the target band and that inflation, with a six to eighteen-month lag, would break out any moment now. Of course that did not happen; M1 grew at over 10 percent a year between 1982 and 1986, and in retrospect it's quite clear that there was a major shift in velocity—an increase in the demand for money—a fact that Milton alluded to earlier when he described his target in terms of M2 rather than M1.

But we should realize that if we are going to choose a target, if we are going to have some degree of commitment to a long-term rule, we are not allowed to pick the rule ex post; we commit to something ahead of time. The switch was in M1 last time, but maybe the shift will be in M2 next time. Bob Mundell, I think, would prefer that the nominal target to which we commit not be M1 or M2 but rather be the exchange rate or the price of gold or the price of a basket of commodities. But that could have the same problem in the future if there is a shift in the demand for money, the demand for gold, or the supply of gold—any of those things. If we target the nominal quantity in question, then we are needlessly transmitting this shift in demand or supply to the entire economy.

Take the example of M1 and do a little calculation, looking at the path of what velocity actually did. What would have happened to nominal GNP if we had rigidly precommitted to M1 the money-growth rule of 3 percent—the rule the Shadow Open Market Committee wanted? The answer is that the maximum rate of growth of nominal GNP from 1982 to 1986 would have been 0.7 percent a year, which, I think, means that the 1982 recession would have lasted another four years. It would have been a truly gratuitous recession, and it's a good thing that Paul Volcker did abandon that target. Well, the exact same thing would be true for the price of gold if there were a shift in the demand for gold or in the supply of gold, and those big shifts do occur.

So that's why my candidate is nominal GNP, with some degree of precommitment to a nominal GNP target. Not absolutely rigid; for international coordination, I have in mind something like the G-7 release at their meetings of what their target rate has been and what it will be for the coming year—perhaps on a yearly basis within a range of plus or minus 1.5 percent; something like that. And if that fails or if, in a national policy-making context, the chairman of the Fed testifies before Congress that he has failed to meet the target, no, you don't fire him or send him out to a firing squad, but he is a little embarrassed. There is a cost because he missed the target.

The advantage of a nominal GNP target is that you won't live to regret it. A nominal target of some kind is all well and good; you get the advantage of reducing inflation expectations. But if it's something that you live to regret because there has been a big shift in demand, the benefit is not much good. My proposal would be both at the national policy-making level and at the level of G-7 coordination. With respect to the G-7, it should focus less on M1 and all the other variables that are now on its list. The G-7 has this list of ten economic indicators that the members negotiate about at their meetings, and nominal GNP is nowhere on that list. I think that's the one variable that they should talk about most. At the present conjuncture, it probably means a slightly higher rate of growth of nominal GNP for the United States— something more like what we had in 1989 rather than what we will probably have this year.

Cooper: So you would urge this particular format on the G-7 now?

Frankel: Yes—both a short-term commitment that would allow for some higher-than-average expansion and a longer-term target that would gradually bring down the growth rate to an appropriate long-term rate.

Issing: That means agreeing on the right model.

Frankel: Well, I think the nominal GNP target is relatively model-free. Some people's view of the Bonn Summit in 1978 is that what went wrong was that the United States had one model in mind and the Germans had another. I think that if you phrase things in terms of nominal GNP rather than M1 or money supply or government spending, the target is relatively robust with respect to uncertainty regarding the correct model, regarding the baseline of the economy today, and regarding future shocks.

Friedman: There's a great deal of sense to what Jeff says. I understand very well the arguments in favor of targeting nominal GNP, and they make sense. But there are two basic defects with this approach. The fundamental problem is, How do you get accountability? How can the people in charge really be kept to the precommitment? There are two possibilities. One is to precommit to something that nobody doubts can be controlled exactly, day to day. That was the advantage under the German system of precommitting to the monetary base. The argument in favor of a base commitment is that there is no question whatsoever that the Federal Reserve has the power to control it from day to day. The other possibility is to have some way of checking up on whether those in charge are somehow or other living up to their commitment.

Now the problem with the nominal GNP target as such is that, in the first place, everybody agrees that it's not something that the Fed controls from day to day. It's something that has a great deal of variability, independently of what the Fed does, especially in the short term. So you can't expect very good results in the short run. But the second problem is that you have to wait a long time before you can see whether the target has been achieved. You have to wait a year or two or three to find out where you are. So the alternative to having the Fed control something that can be determined from day to day is to have some mechanism—some indication on a daily, weekly, monthly basis—that will show whether the Fed is doing its job properly.

That's the enormous virtue of a proposal under which the U.S. government would issue purchasing-power bonds in addition to securities of the present variety. This would provide a way of checking up on whether the Fed is performing its job day by day, week by week, month by month in the form of a market estimate of the anticipated rate of inflation. What you want the Fed to do is to keep the anticipated rate of inflation low. And if it keeps the interest rates on the two types of bonds within three percentage points, the Fed is doing just that. If the spread gets widely outside that range, the Fed is not doing its job.

This is a perfectly feasible proposal. It's not my straight monetary-growth method at all. It's a method that allows the Fed to have all the discretion in the world, but which provides a day-to-day market estimate of the Fed's degree of success in coping with inflationary pressures. It is highly desirable for the U.S. government to issue purchasing-power securities for other reasons, so you're killing two birds with one stone. And I'm suggesting that this is a proposal that has not been really widely discussed and which I think is a more promising approach than trying to target nominal GNP.

Now all this has to do with domestic policy. So far as international coordination is concerned, my view on that is very simple. I think that international coordination does a great deal of harm, that it never does any good, and that there ought not to be any. Individual countries ought to be responsible for themselves. If each country behaves properly in terms of its own interests, you will get the most effective kind of international coordination, which is through the market.

Johnson: I just want to say that Milton is absolutely right about nominal GNP. We've been trying in the United Kingdom to operate a nominal GNP target for the last six years, and look at our economy today!

Cooper: But is it because you missed the target? Maybe you can elaborate on that.

Johnson: The approach has various objections. First, nobody knew how to achieve a particular nominal GNP target. Second, nobody could measure what the nominal GNP was until about a year after it happened, and the figure kept on being revised, usually upward, until long after the event.

Issing: I am much in sympathy with Milton's last remark on policy coordination. I am less in sympathy with his remarks on what central banks should do. He is even more hostile toward me than I had supposed [loud laughter]. I have been a board member of the Bundesbank now for three months, and if I had been held responsible for everything connected with monetary policy on a day-to-day or week-to-week basis, I would already have been dismissed from my appointment and would never have rented a flat in Frankfurt [more laughter].

But, to come back to GNP targeting, my main problem with this approach is implementation. Suppose your target for nominal GNP growth is 5 percent, and you see that the consumer-price index has risen by 5 percent; that reflects what has happened in the past. So now what do you do? Suppress the money-growth rate? So, why don't you follow a money-growth rule?

Frankel: Because of velocity.

Issing: Yes, you suppress money supply. But how much? Your rule doesn't help. I think it brings you into the problems of discretionary policy. You will have a lot of overshooting and undershooting, because your target doesn't help you in the implementation problem.

Krugman: It's striking that neither Jeff nor anyone else has said much about the case for international coordination. Milton Friedman has delivered a verdict against it but has not offered an argument for that verdict.

Friedman: You have to give me the argument.

Krugman: I know, I was afraid you would say that. Let me talk about the coordination case for a minute, because that is in fact what we should be talking about. What should the G-7 ministers have been doing? There's an academic argument for policy coordination—the argument we like to make—which is that there are externalities, that there are spill-overs between countries' national monetary policies. Suppose that you've got inflation around the world; whether it's the result of a recent supply shock or inherited inflation from past bad policies doesn't matter. The simple argument is that each country has an incentive to pursue a particularly tight monetary policy because it gets an extra disinflationary kick out of an exchange-rate appreciation. But of course if they all do that, they can't all get the exchange-rate appreciation, so they get caught in a kind of prisoner's dilemma in which everyone pursues an excessively rapid disinflation. It's in the interest of the countries to coordinate so that they don't do that.

But when people try to estimate the gains from this kind of coordination, they always come up with embarrassingly small numbers because the only way you can estimate it is to try to infer from countries' actual behavior what their preferences are. And if you do that, you find that during the 1980s, during the period of heroic disinflation, countries really cared an awful lot about fighting inflation. They cared so much about it that the effect of their coordinated efforts under G-7 arrangements was not very great. And in fact I suppose a lot of people around this table—not me, by the way—would say that countries must always be even more disinflationary than they would be anyway, so the bias in policy that may come out of coordination failures may actually be all to the good.

But is any of that relevant now? I find it very hard to come up with anything about the current situation that would suggest that there are strong externalities from policy coordination. I don't think that there is any kind of prisoner's dilemma aspect that is really a serious constraint on policy or is seriously biasing policies of any of the G-3. The other four of the G-7 have problems with their neighbors, perhaps, but those can be handled on a regional basis. As far as I can make out, the actual G-7 process was based on an extended version of what some people at the Federal Reserve call the "slap-in-the-face" theory of intervention, which is that the foreign-exchange market occasionally goes crazy and we at the Fed know better, so by intervening against the market, we can sort of force the market to behave the way we want it to. And the market, if we've done it right, stops and says, Thanks, I needed that. The idea is that those slaps in the face are more effective if administered by several countries at once, so they can convince the market that one central bank could be wrong, but seven can't.

Frankel: Like the 1985 Plaza agreement on exchange rates.

Krugman: Yes, Plaza and then the Louvre agreement—both.

Friedman: The Louvre agreement was more important.

Krugman: Well, in both cases. The Plaza idea was that the market was overvaluing the dollar and that we could bring it to its senses. The Louvre idea was that the dollar was falling too fast and that we could convince the market that it was wrong. And for a time this seemed to work. In fact, one of the great puzzles has been the extraordinary influence that the G-7 seemed to have for a little while with very little fundamental policy backup. But again, whether you think that was a good thing or not—I guess I think it was a moderately good thing, but relatively small in the scale of things—that influence is now pretty much gone. I don't know what they did at their last meeting—it's hard to imagine that they did much of anything—but I guess it's hard to get very upset about that.

Mundell: Well, I certainly favor coordination in the sense at least of sharing information of the kind used by the G-7. It helps a lot for countries to talk over their policies, explain them, and perhaps in the process change them. It's another thing if countries actually have to follow a policy that they think is against their interests. I agree with Milton that each country, when it's not doing particular harm to other countries, should follow its own self-interest. But the question then is, When countries follow their own self-interest, does that implicitly involve a high degree of coordination? Under the Bretton Woods system, the United States pegged to gold and other countries pegged to the dollar. That implied coordination, even if it was a one-sided and asymmetrical coordination. But countries that adopted this system believed in it and believed that it suited their self-interest.

Now the question is, If you do believe in some kind of coordination, what should the target be? I agree with Milton that targeting nominal GNP is not a feasible objective. Targeting the monetary base or nominal reserves is a different thing, but I think this is too loose a way of getting to the goals that we want, because there is too much slippage between the ratio of reserves to money and there are too many definitions of what money is. My preference is exchange-rate targeting, where countries peg to the currency of a country with a stable price level. I know that Milton Friedman, in a very insightful paper in 1975, recommended that Yugoslavia peg its currency to the D-mark on the ground that the German monetary authorities were more highly qualified, were better, than the Yugoslav monetary authorities. Germany had an excellent track record, and it did make sense for a country that didn't have such a record to choose stability in this way.

As far as coordination is concerned, if we had a system of stable exchange rates and if we had a big country like the United States with a stable currency, then I do think that this would be the best system of coordination that we could possibly achieve. Now as we move toward the idea of a monetary area in Europe, we will end up with two big floating blocs: the dollar area and either the wider D-mark area as it is now or a genuine European currency area with a common European currency. We will then have to decide what the exchange-rate policies between these two large areas will be. I think it would be extremely foolhardy for any economist ever to suggest, once this European area is created, that either the central bank of Europe or the central bank of the United States could afford to be indifferent about the exchange rate—this most fundamental of prices in the system. It's such a vital price; it's more important now, of course, than the price of gold.

Now I'll say one last thing. Jeffrey mentioned my attraction to gold, which at the moment has become unstable. The reason why gold was a very stable asset historically was because it was very widely held in individual hands. It is no longer widely held; it's held mainly by central banks—a billion ounces by central banks and perhaps another billion ounces in speculative deposits. Now Europe has 600 million of these ounces; the United States has about 250 million of them. Europe has a dominating and controlling voice, potentially, if it wanted to exercise it, over the existing gold market. And the central banks of the world have a twenty-year supply, annual supply, of gold.

So gold policy does become relevant. I remember that at every one of the conferences that Randall has held, gold was considered an important subject to discuss. Central banks hold $400 billion of this asset, and it seems to me that nobody can talk about the future direction of the international monetary system without saying something about gold. I don't think that we can move toward a gold standard of the old type, but somehow or other gold has to be brought into the discussion.

Cooper: When you say "has to be brought into the discussion," do you mean that there has to be a disposal strategy? Gold is on the balance sheets now; it serves no useful function, and therefore we have to . . .

Mundell [interrupting]:   No, no, there has to be a disposal strategy for the question. We have to deal with it. How should we deal with the gold question? I know you think we should throw it all away.

Cooper: Optimally.

Mundell: John Williamson thinks that we should give it all away to the less-developed countries, or a large fraction of it. I know that view is shared by a lot of people. The traditional argument against any use of gold for monetary purposes are that South Africa produces most of it and that the Soviet Union is the country that has most of the world's below-ground stock of gold reserves. But because of recent changes in both countries, that argument has far less force today.

Solomon: As others before me, I was going to make a case for policy coordination after Milton Friedman's critical remark, but Paul Krugman and Bob Mundell, in the early part of his statement, have done it. When Bob moved halfway through his remarks, I began diverging from him. But I won't try to repeat the case for the international coordination of macro policies except to make two points, if I may, to Milton and others.

First, Milton said that countries, instead of coordinating, ought to follow their self-interest. The obvious point—as you know very well, Milton—is that a country's self-interest depends upon what other countries are going to do. So your assertion against coordination isn't a sufficient disposal of the issue. The externalities, the spill-overs that Paul Krugman mentioned are part of what policymakers have to take into account when they decide on policies, assuming that one is willing to live with discretionary policies. That's point number one.

Point number two: people say, Well, what did the G-7 do the last time they met? But this process of policy coordination does not require continuous adjustment of policy. It's a sort of standby arrangement whereby policymakers, while they monitor continuously, don't have to act continuously every time they meet. They do need to act occasionally, as in the circumstances Paul mentioned, when they might otherwise all overreact to an external shock, such as an oil-price increase, or when there are other disturbances to their economies that require taking these spill-overs into account. But that doesn't mean continuous action.

Willet: I would like to move back to Milton's comment on Jeff Frankel's case for targeting nominal GNP. I come in very much on the side of the need for accountability, so Jeff's mechanism—that if you miss your GNP target, you will be slightly embarrassed—is not quite as strong as I would like to see. Personally, I would favor a lot more work on the case for longer-term nominal GNP as a target, where what the monetary authorities are held accountable for is hitting some kind of longer-term average over a period of several years, within some margin. I think it would be very useful to know whether such an approach is feasible and enforceable.

I understand that the central bank of New Zealand is now having an interesting experiment in which the governor is making a long-term commitment to meet some long-term targets, with his job apparently at stake. I think there may be a number of institutional forms involving longer-term commitments that could be explored. The monetary authorities could be permitted to have a degree of discretion, and if the target is a longer-term average of some kind, probably none of us would be terribly upset if the target were missed for a year or two, as long as the divergence didn't keep getting bigger. One might differ on whether this is optimal, but it wouldn't be terribly upsetting. On the other hand, if the target is missed in the same direction over a number of years, that's when you start to worry about inflationary or deflationary bias.

Friedman: But if you wait for a long-run agreement with the target, Keynes was right about that: In the long run, we're all dead.

Willett: What about medium term?

Friedman: What is it—three years? So three years after they've made a mistake, you know they've made a mistake.

Willett: Yes.

Friedman: Then you wait another three years for them to correct it, because, after all, you can't expect them to correct it overnight. I also want to comment on what Bob Mundell said. It ties in very closely with another issue that we have on the agenda for tomorrow—the question of the monetary system for Eastern Europe. Bob referred to my article on Yugoslavia in the context of a much more general position that I have long held, which is that the optimum monetary system for most small countries is not to peg, but to unify their currencies with the currency of a large country.

Cooper: Luxembourg, for example.

Friedman: That's right. I mean unified: Panama with the dollar, Hong Kong with the dollar—not Chile with the dollar, where it was pegged; not Israel with the dollar, where it was pegged. Those were very different cases.

Now I come to another idea that I don't think has received enough consideration. What would be the optimum monetary system for Poland right now? In my opinion, the optimum thing for Poland to do would be to institute a new zloty, perhaps with another name. It's like the Hong Kong system. What you do is this: You say that here's a new Polish currency that has the property that the only way it can be created is that you deposit, say, two marks plus one dollar, and you get back X new zlotys. These marks and dollars are kept in a fund in a foreign bank with a board of directors or group of trustees in charge consisting partly of Polish people and partly of foreign bankers. This new zloty is free to float with respect to the old zloty in an open market—there are no controls on that—and people can create as many of these new zlotys as they wish. What you have is the extreme case of a gold standard—actually a mark-dollar standard—set up in such a way that Poland collects the seigniorage on it.

Cooper: The currency-board system.

Friedman: It's a currency-board system; that's why I referred to Hong Kong. There's no political control over the quantity of money, and the Poles achieve the objective of linking a bad monetary system to a good one. That is to say, I don't think the Polish monetary authorities are going to do nearly as well as the Bundesbank; they won't even do as well as the Fed. The Bundesbank would have done still better if it hadn't been for the perverse pressures that the Fed put on it. But it seems to me that the monetary arrangement I've described would be the most sensible system for countries like Poland, Yugoslavia, Czechoslovakia, and Hungary. Now, in my view, if they are not willing to do that and if they insist on having independent central banks, the only alternative that makes sense is a completely floating exchange rate—nothing else. I think that the pegged system, the system of pegging your currency to another while retaining an independent monetary policy, is worse than either extreme.

Mundell: Well, what you propose is a peg, though, with 100 percent reserves behind it.

Friedman: This is a peg with 100 percent reserves, but it's a unified currency, fundamentally, as opposed to a pegged currency.

Cooper: And as you've described it, it's a parallel currency. But what I'd like to do is rule that this particular topic, which is fascinating, should be discussed tomorrow, because I think we want to come back to the question of currency arrangements among Eastern countries and whether there should be parallel currencies or currency boards or whatever.

But now I would like, Milton, to tweak you a little bit on the question of policy coordination. As I understood you, you said that there is no scope for it, and indeed, I thought you said that it always does damage and that it's much better for a country to pursue its own interests.

Friedman: On the whole, coordination does worse.

Cooper: What I'm wondering is whether you're making an empirical or a theoretical statement. Let me pose a proposition that I think you will agree with, which is that even when countries pursue what they think are their own interests, by your standards they do it badly. But they do it differently badly. Might there not be some scope under those circumstances for policy coordination as a means of improving welfare? And if not, why not?

Friedman: My point is entirely empirical and not theoretical. I have no quarrel whatsoever with the theoretical argument. There are spillovers that in principle favor coordinated policy, but my argument is from a political, not an economic, point of view. And from a political point of view, I find it intolerable that anything important for a country should be decided in a forum that is not politically responsible to that country.

The problem is that you have these people at the G-7, for example, who have not only their country's economic interests at stake but also their own political interests at stake. They're politicians; they're pursuing some political interest. I have no reason to believe that the political externalities in this process of coordination are in any way identical with the economic externalities. And when I observe what actually happens, I see that the Plaza agreement had little effect, except very temporarily. I see that the Louvre agreement did a good deal of harm, because in the year before that agreement, the capital inflow into the United States was nearly 100 percent private, whereas in the year after the agreement, 75 percent of it was governmental, which meant that it was impeding the adjustments that would have taken place as a result of the gradually declining dollar exchange rate. And with Japan and Germany in a position where they had accumulated all the dollars they were willing to swallow, a sharp break in the exchange rate was the outcome. So I say that the Louvre agreement did a great deal of harm. I don't know of any international coordination effort that has worked. Give me one example.

Cooper: The EMS is an international coordination mechanism, and depending on one's preferences, some people say it has worked very importantly for France. You can disagree about that, but the disagreement is over preferences, not over whether the EMS had an impact on

French policy. I think there's no doubt that it did have an impact on French policy.

Friedman: It may have; I'm not sure it did. The empirical evidence is not as clear as you make it out to be.

Cooper: Neither is it on the Louvre agreement. I'm using the same standard exactly—neither stronger nor weaker than you used in your example.

Krugman: On trade policy, most of us—I don't know what Milton thinks—but most of us think that the GATT on the whole has led to better trade policies on the part of participants. That was another group of people with political and economic interests representing their respective countries, and I, at least, think that the political externalities there were favorable. That doesn't settle the question; I actually find the case for monetary coordination dubious, myself, but there's not a blanket rule that says that international negotiation over policies is a bad thing.

Friedman: No, I'm not going to say it's a bad thing every single time; I'm going to say that in the great bulk of cases I believe that the attempt to coordinate is a bad thing.

Krugman: Only on monetary issues or on all issues?

Friedman: No, I'm including trade negotiations. I have always favored unilateral movements toward freer trade over these kinds of . . .

Cooper [interrupting]: And how many have you seen?

Friedman: Well, look. You had the GATT, but you also had the textile agreement, and you had the so-called voluntary export quotas. The GATT did not prevent widespread movement toward protectionism. And it's not entirely clear to me that if there had never been a GATT, you would have had a more protectionist world than you've had. That's not a self-evident proposition.

Cooper: No counter-factual statement is self-evident; that's a valid generalization.

Solomon: Well, there are all sorts of policy coordination. We're now discussing trade policy. We started off, I thought, on macro policy coordination, and Milton's castigation was with respect to exchange-rate policy coordination. But his clarifying remarks were very interesting. He said he accepts the theoretical case for macroeconomic policy coordination; he accepts what Paul Krugman, Jeff Frankel, and I were saying about spillovers, externalities, and so on. I did have trouble with his reference to political intolerability. If I understand you, Milton, is that just another way of saying that you don't believe in discretionary policy? I don't understand you if that's not what you mean.

Frankel: "No taxation without representation."

Friedman: That's right.

Solomon: That's what you're saying; you don't believe in discretionary policy.

Friedman: No taxation without representation.

Solomon: But there *is* representation. You yourself said that the people who sit at the Group of Seven are finance ministers and central bank governors; they're the ones who make the policy decisions for their own countries, based on what they've learned about the policy intentions of the other six countries. They have the political responsibility; that's taxation *with* representation. What's wrong with that?

Friedman: They're going to use their positions to try to see if they can't induce the other countries to behave against their interests where that will redound to the interests of their own countries and their own political positions.

Solomon: So am I right when I say your case is really the case against discretionary policy?

Friedman: Absolutely.

Solomon: Okay, I understand you.

Issing: As to Milton's remark on the GATT, I just want to say that one has to differentiate between discretion and rules. It is true that the GATT hasn't hampered the existence of the textile agreement, and so on, but it has set rules for a kind of free trade and for sanctions when the rules are violated, and for this reason coordination make sense. You don't get this without international agreements. You can't do it on a bilateral basis, because governments change, and so the next day you might have a different trade policy. So we need coordination for establishing rules.

6.

Monetary Issues in Western Europe

Introduced by Christopher Johnson

Chairman Cooper: There are a number of loose ends from yesterday, but I thought this morning we should start with monetary developments in Western Europe. I do not mean now the German fiscal situation, which we discussed yesterday, but the longer-run monetary plans for Europe. We'll see how that discussion goes, but my thought is that it will evolve into a discussion of the second issue raised by Bob Mundell, which is regionalism—what it means, what the prospects are, whether there's anything to it, what the advantages and disadvantages are—and then reserve our discussion of Eastern European developments for this afternoon, plus some miscellany left over from yesterday of things we haven't touched on at all, but perhaps ought to before the session is over. If that's agreeable, I will ask Christopher Johnson to lead off on the discussion of European monetary union, just to get the topic on the table in a systematic way.

Johnson: Thank you very much, Mr. Chairman. Well now, you know that I'm a Brit—you can all tell by the accent who the Brits are around here—but today I'm speaking as a European. And there are two of us. We speak in slightly different accents, but I expect it all sounds the same to you people. (Your accents all sound the same to us, although I know there are certain regional differences which the Professor Higginses of this world are good at spotting.) So let me try to give a European view. I've set out a ten-point plan which some of you may have seen. I'm going to give myself just under half a minute for each point, and then we can take up some of them later if that's agreeable to the chairman.

Now the first point I want to make is that we are trying to create a proper single market in Europe—the 1992 program. And I believe that it's possible to have a unified market only if you also have a single currency. Exchange-rate changes are perhaps the biggest remaining nontariff barrier to trade. One market implies one price, and if you have not only one price but one currency, then pricing becomes transparent, and everybody can see much more easily what everything costs in different parts of the market. This is true above all for the banking industry. We shan't get true competition in the banking industry as long as interest-rate differences are dominated by expected exchange-rate changes rather than by differences in the underlying efficiency of different banks' operations.

The second point I want to make is that a single currency is vastly preferable to so-called irrevocably fixed exchange rates. It's impossible to fix exchange rates irrevocably because of the problem we have learned to call that of "time-inconsistency." It in fact pays governments in certain circumstances to undertake not to change their exchange rate, and then to do so when the markets are least expecting it. A single currency is also preferable from the point of view of reducing transactions costs. Many of the transactions costs due to multiple currencies are not only those relating to uncertain exchange rates but those of having to convert accounts, of having different computer systems, and so on.

My third point is that the single currency we have to have will almost certainly be called the ecu, which stands for European currency unit. It will not be called the deutsche mark, even if one thinks that the ecu will in fact be the deutsche mark in sheep's clothing. But this is an important presentational point. The Germans, for sound political reasons, are the last people who would want to impose a currency called the deutsche mark on the rest of Europe. If we can have an ecu as good as the deutsche mark, then Germany will not have lost anything, and the rest of us will have gained something. Britain has proposed a hard ecu plan which essentially says, Let's make the ecu worth at least as much as the strongest European currency—which we all expect to be the deutsche mark.

Point number four. We have to agree on the destination of monetary union; we have to agree that it does mean a single currency and not some other kind of regime. The British originally wasted a certain amount of time, or should I say played for a certain amount of time, until we could give Mrs. Thatcher an honorable farewell, which we have now done. So we can now agree that it was no good saying, Let's have currency competition.

This leads me to my next point, which is factual. It's not true that good money always drives out bad. If the interest rate on bad money is higher and the exchange rate is fixed, then bad money may drive out good. There's an awful lot of sterling around at the moment on which you can get an interest rate of 14 percent, and from that point of view—the point of view of inflation—sterling is rather a bad money, a weak currency, but it certainly hasn't been driven out in present circumstances.

My sixth point is that if you have a monetary union, you must have a common monetary policy. This implies not only that nominal interest rates should reflect only credit differences, but that you must in fact have the common monetary policy run by some kind of central institution.

And here we come to my seventh point, which is that we have to have some kind of European central banking system which is independent of political pressure in the way the Bundesbank is independent and, I think, the Fed nearly always is. But the first stage toward this would be to make the national central banks independent of their government, as a prelude to their merging their independences into one European central bank, which would be accountable probably to the Council of Economics and Finance Ministers as well as to the European Parliament and, indeed, to national parliaments—why not?

Point number eight is that, having unified our monetary policies, we can still retain a good deal of national fiscal diversity. This doesn't mean that anything goes. It doesn't mean that deficit countries can increase borrowing and know that it's guaranteed by the monetary union. There should be rules to prevent monetary financing of deficits. It should still be possible to allow countries great latitude in how they raise their tax revenues, what balance they have between acting on the expenditure side and the taxation side, but bearing in mind that if, say, Germany at the moment were to go on borrowing without limit, even though it's a soundly run country, this would raise long-term interest rates throughout the monetary union and thus would be of concern to everybody, not only Germany.

My ninth point is that of course the membership of the United Kingdom is essential for European monetary union to proceed. If one can talk about monetary union on a narrower basis, this would be a very bad split in the existing Economic Community. It could only be tolerated as a very temporary measure, if that. And I think that the United Kingdom will be ready to join some kind of second stage of the monetary union by the beginning of 1992, the date which is now being canvassed, because, by then, if we haven't got our inflation rate down to 4 or 5 percent, God help us. And indeed one reason we joined the European Monetary System was to help us get inflation down, and there is already some sign that the exchange-rate discipline, the credibility of the system, is having effects on British wage-bargaining behavior, which is as it should be and, indeed, as it has been in other member countries.

My final, tenth point is that one cannot escape the need for some kind of political union as an adjunct to a monetary union. We've talked about having a single central banking organization, and indeed there must be other kinds of economic policy coordination. But political union as now discussed in Europe does not necessarily mean a federation. To some people it does, but the United States is certainly not the only model one can have for a monetary union and close commercial and economic cooperation. The European Community is sui generis; it is based on the belief that you can pool sovereignty for some purposes but not necessarily for others. That may come later. We certainly don't seem to be near pooling our sovereignty on defense just yet—one of the lessons of the Iraqi war. But it should be possible for us to pool our monetary sovereignty, run a successful monetary union, and thus make a success of a true common market without tariff or nontariff barriers to trade. And when we look at the way in which the United Kingdom has used or abused its monetary sovereignty over the last twenty years, I think we could all agree that we would be better off without it.

Cooper: Thank you very much, Christopher. You alluded in your remarks to stage two of the EMU. Some of us may not be completely versed in the stages. Do you want to tell us factually about the stages that at least you have in mind?

Johnson: Right. Well, these are the stages put forward in the Delors Report by the president of the Common Market Commission. Stage one consists in all countries joining the exchange-rate mechanism, or EMS, of the European Monetary System, fixing their exchange rates within 2.25 percent bands (we are still at 6 percent bands). So some time in the next year or two in stage one, we have to come to 2.25 percent bands.

Now stage two is at the moment under discussion, and I think it will mean something like agreeing not to realign exchange rates if at all possible. It's something like irrevocably fixed exchange rates, except that everybody knows that irrevocable is true only up to a point—maybe allowing time for countries like Greece and Portugal to join the stage one exchange-rate mechanism and in the meantime promoting the use of the ecu and giving Europe an embryo European central bank. We already have a committee of central bank governors giving this organization some kind of power to manage and develop the ecu and, indeed, prepare for stage three, which is full monetary union and which I think now has to mean a common currency.

But the common currency could have different identifications. In the United States, for example, you have New York dollars, Richmond dollars, and San Francisco dollars. You could have a British ecu and a French ecu, and in the coinage they could be called the pound and the franc. They could be either at par with each other or at totally fixed rates, like three to one for the D-mark and the pound. So when I say a single currency, there are shadings here to allow for at least paying lip service to national political identities. As for stage three, we're thinking that this could be any time between 1997 and 2000, but 2000 looks like a good millenial kind of date to aim for.

Sven W. Arndt: Christopher, as you know, there are those who say that the real side of adjustment—the completion of the internal market—would generate significant real shocks and disturbances as markets get consolidated and resources get moved around. This suggests to some at least that before you fix exchange rates, you ought to wait until you've looked at what the real side of the market will yield.

Johnson: Yes, I think this is a question we dealt with a bit yesterday— Are countries ready to renounce the devaluation option? Is that a more painless way of dealing with shocks? There are people in Britain who think we shouldn't give up the devaluation weapon just yet. And indeed as long as we have stage one and the possibility of realignments, nobody has given up the devaluation. But what you are faced with is the fact that the behavior of agents in the economy is very much a function, not just of the kind of regime they are living in, but of the kind of regime they perceive they are living in. And if it's clear to trade-union bargainers that there is no possibility of exchange-rate adjustment, then I think experience shows that their bargaining behavior is substantially changed, and therefore you don't get the same kind of real shock in terms of unemployment, let's say, that you would have if you had a regime of fixed but adjustable exchange rates, even where you decide not to adjust the rates. This is, in fact, quite different from having truly fixed exchange rates or, better still, a common currency. But I have to say that we are still all learning here, and I'm not sure how much the past models help, except the model of what has actually been happening in the exchange-rate mechanism in the last ten years, particularly in the case of France.

Cooper: Would it be fair to say that, in your opinion, the gamble is that there basically won't be any real shocks that come out of completing the integration of the market? The one example you gave was about national wage settlements and your inference that the existence of a common market in goods and services and the prospect or expectation of a common currency will eliminate, or at least greatly attenuate, that particular source of shock.

Johnson: Well, let's say I think the effect of many of the shocks is likely to be more on regions than on countries, and if you wanted to use the devaluation weapon, you should really be devaluating the Welsh pound against the English pound, or something like that. Devaluating a national currency doesn't help a regional problem within that currency area.

Mundell: I didn't notice in your ten points whether all countries should move toward the targets at the same time or whether they should move in sequence, beginning with those countries that are ready for it.

Johnson: Yes, I referred to that briefly when describing stage two, saying it might be possible for countries like Greece and Portugal, which still have some way to go on inflation convergence, to join later. Some people think Britain should join later, but I think that would be a tactical error at the very least and not necessary if we have inflation convergence by the time stage two begins.

What I think we are seeing at the moment is that countries are choosing a time to declare that they will not use the realignment weapon. Belgium has already committed itself to never again realign against the D-mark. Now of course that is subject to "time-inconsistency." Nevertheless, most people accept that they are able to do that in present circumstances. It might be amusing if suddenly they were faced with the possibility of having to realign upward against the D-mark. We discussed that case yesterday, but it's on balance unlikely. The French haven't quite formally renounced the realignment weapon, but they have made it clear that they would not want a realignment against the D-mark. And I think the Germans on the whole have accepted that, although maybe Otmar has a different view.

Mundell: The big worrisome country—not talking about Spain, Portugal, or Greece—is Italy with its 10 percent budget deficit. Italy will have to have some kind of fiscal reform before it can renounce the devaluation option. Just recently, asset prices in Italy have leaped up, probably in anticipation of a realignment or the possibility of a realignment. And if that realignment doesn't take place, then Italy is going to get stuck with a very uncompetitive price structure.

Johnson: Well, I think there are two problems facing Italy. One, as you say, is the inflation rate; it's now about 6 percent. That was our inflation rate last year, but ours is expected to go down, whereas Italy's is not. But, I think in Italy the traded-goods sector and its prices do behave in a substantially different way from consumer prices, which include services. And I don't think one should be too carried away by crude CPI comparisons. Japan is another example where the price level of traded goods behaves quite differently and goes down while other prices go up. But the fiscal problem in Italy is serious, and I think the Italians might well accept some pressure from other members of the union to sort out their fiscal situation. As you know from the way the International Monetary Fund works, or used to work, in the case of Italy among others, having external pressure can be quite useful to the government in trying to get things done.

Mundell: Yes. May I go on with a couple of questions related to that? In the scheme for introducing the new ecu, do you have in mind calling in the old currencies and replacing with the ecus? They could coexist side by side.

Johnson: I think one of the main differences between Germany and not only Britain, but France and some of the other countries as well, is whether one should promote the use of the ecu as a parallel currency and also a common currency before it becomes the single currency. There is a danger that you might have excessive currency creation, but you could of course step down your creation of other national currencies to compensate. I think most of us feel that it's a good idea to have a sort of learning process to accustom people to the ecu, to see what prices look like in ecu, as a preparatory stage before you simply replace all the national currencies with the ecu.

Cooper: What does that mean in practice—that if you go into a shop everything has two prices?

Johnson: Well, some companies think that would be a very fine idea, because it could be associated with a form of inflation accounting. They did try an ecu week in Luxembourg last year; all the shop prices were in ecu and in Belgolux francs. And you can of course write out checks in ecu now if people will accept them. I think that would be more for commercial operations; companies would quote each other prices in ecu. Some of them do that now. Bureaucrats would get their salaries in ecu.

Cooper: But could they spend them?

Johnson: Well, they might have to convert them; they would be converting them at par at an agreed parity for some other currency. All this will take a bit of time, and I think it might be better to do it gradually than to have the "big bang" approach, which is the other route Bob Mundell referred to.

Mundell: It seems to me difficult—the gradual approach. There are two big problems. The first question is, At what point will the ecu become legal tender? And second, At what point will the national currencies cease to be legal tender? These steps could be taken simultaneously, though the second step involves tossing out what is historically a very important part of national sovereignty, especially for a country like Britain, which has had the pound for over a thousand years.

Johnson: Well, of course, national currencies would only cease to be legal tender on the day you withdrew them—that's fairly clear. There's a big argument about whether the ecu needs to become legal tender in order to be an acceptable international currency in financing trade at this stage. And nobody quite knows what legal tender means. I think it means being able to turn a bank deposit into bank notes and coins, and until you have ecu bank notes, I don't see how the ecu can be legal tender.

Mundell: Can you pay taxes with ecu?

Johnson: No, I think paying taxes is a different point.

Cooper: Legal tender means that the creditor cannot refuse payment. That's critical, even at the shop level. It means the creditor cannot refuse payment in X, where X is legal tender.

Johnson: Yes, that's one definition of legal tender; I don't think it's the only one. For example, Scottish pound notes are legal tender in Britain, but cab drivers often refuse to accept them. So what do you do—haul them off to the police station?

Cooper: You can do that.

Johnson: Yes, but it's a question of commercial acceptability and not just of what is or is not legal tender.

Cooper: But since you're paying at the end of the cab ride and not at the beginning, the customer has the upper hand. The cab driver can refuse the Scottish pound note, but that's tantamount to saying he's doing the job for nothing.

Johnson: Yes, yes, right.

Mundell: I have one last question in this round. Would you exclude from your discussion the possibility of having the Bundesbank convert the D-mark into the ecu? For example, the Bundesbank could buy up all the other currencies with D-marks that could be renamed ecus.

Johnson: Well, I know that my friend Sam Brittan would say that this was perfectly acceptable to him; he would be happy to have the D-mark as our common currency. I think there are one or two disadvantages in addition to the political one I mentioned. One reason why countries like France are keen on a genuine monetary union is that they want to have some influence on the policy of the Bundesbank. They want to be able to influence it in the direction of economic activity as opposed to inflation fighting. And this, I think, is one reason why the Germans are a little bit suspicious of some of the plans that have been put forward, because they see them as involving some sacrifice of the independence of the Bundesbank vis-à-vis other central banks and perhaps vis-à-vis the European politicians. Maybe Otmar would like to comment on that.

Willett: The stage two procedures have worried a number of us in the sense that a worst-case scenario would be to decide to lock in your exchange rates and then hope that policy coordination will follow. The EMS has worked surprisingly well, but one can at least argue that this was due in part to favorable sets of circumstances and similar objectives at particular times. What impresses me is that a great deal of the optimism that prevails rests on the discipline that the Bundesbank will provide as an example. But, as Christopher just mentioned, the French would like to have more control over the central bank arrangements in the EMU, so I wonder what the prospects are for a truly independent central bank that would more approximate the Bundesbank than the Bank of France.

Solomon: Christopher talked a little bit about fiscal diversity among the members, but he didn't say anything about any sort of central fiscal authority. What provisions are there in a system of fixed exchange rates to help smooth out regional changes in economic activity and to deal with regional shocks?

Cooper: You're asking about international fiscal transfers within the Community?

Solomon: Exactly.

Issing: I have a number of points. I don't want to start with a family quarrel in Europe.

Cooper: No, that's a good place to start. You should not be inhibited here from talking about these family quarrels.

Issing: First, let me say that I am not in favor of achieving European monetary integration at two rates of speed: a faster speed for one group of countries and a slower speed for a less qualified group. That would split countries into first-class and second-class members. The risk is that countries, let's say like Italy, wouldn't agree to being downgraded, and that would cause great friction from the beginning.

I think that currency union with one single currency makes sense only if one is prepared to move toward political union. For me it doesn't make sense to have a single currency for a politically diversified Europe. My personal fear is that politicians will agree on having a single currency and on nothing else. In my view, currency union should not precede political union. First, member countries must be willing to give up sovereignty to a *real* European Parliament, to a European government.

A European market does not require a European currency. We can have a free flow of goods, services, and capital without even having fixed exchange rates. But I think it would be a good thing for Europe to move in the direction of monetary integration and perhaps at some stage to have a single currency, but of course it shouldn't be called the deutsche mark. We all agree on this, and it's a rather clever invention to call the currency unit an ecu, because for the British it means European currency unit and for France it means ecu, which was a French coin from former days. So that problem has been neatly solved.

But the point is how to get from here to the single currency. There is agreement that the success of the EMS has come, in considerable part at least, from the anchor function of the deutsche mark. And of course as you move toward stage three, the D-mark loses this function, and we have to decide what we need to do if we don't have this anchor.

What is the alternative? Where does the new regime get its credibility? You gain credibility only by good policy, and gaining credibility in this way takes time. I think that before going to the final step, Europe has to show that it can manage stable currencies without having the D-mark as an anchor. And this must be tested by the markets.

Politicians are pushing this process at a very fast rate. In the communiqué of the meeting of heads of state in Rome, it was announced that on January 1, 1994, we must have a new institution. Of course, you know how such communiqués are worked out during the night; somebody brings it in, and the participants don't notice all the details because they're tired. But now they're asking, What does this mean— the new institution? France, of course, says it means a new European central bank. And the Germans—most Germans—say, no, we never thought of having a European central bank as early as the beginning of 1994. We now have twelve European central banks (eleven without Luxemburg); why do we need an additional European central bank? But I suppose we will have this institution, and from past history we know that the institution will find something to do. But the combination of having twelve national currencies, twelve national central banks, an ecu, and a new institution is an unattractive prospect for me. Why do we need a thirteenth currency? As a central banker, I've quite some sympathy with the idea of currency competition, but competition among national currencies.

Of course the ecu is already in existence, and the private ecu, which has been used for bond issues and loans, is quite successful. But for this you don't need a new institution. Any bank can exchange ecus for a bundle of currencies. That's the private ecu. The official ecu up to now hasn't been useful in any sense, and all agree. But now the idea is to create a "hard ecu," which means that it would be at least as good as the best national currency. Initially, it would be a parallel currency.

But the hard ecu plan makes life very complicated. If, say, an amount of hard ecu equal to 10 percent of the national money supplies is created, what would that mean, for example, for our German monetary target? Should we say the same target minus 10 percent? Of course we don't know how much ecu would come in from the ecu market, so monetary policy would be very, very difficult. And after the creation of the new institution, we might have the situation where, in the morning, the governors of the national central banks would meet in Basel as national central bank representatives, while in the afternoon, the same people would meet as representatives of the new institution, doing ecu business. I think that would create a lot of confusion.

So I think that going from here to currency union will take considerable time. There must be a convergence of inflation rates and a narrowing of interest-rate differentials, a process that may last for years. Then, some day, I think we can have a real common currency.

Conrad C. Jamison: If we miss the year 2000, there's 3000.

Issing: It all depends on good policies.

Cooper: You said a precondition, a necessary condition, for European monetary union in your view is political union, and you gave some reasons. Christopher did not disagree with that, but he made the point that there are many forms of political union, and one need not think just of a federation, such as the United States. I think it would be useful to go precisely to this question of the probability of that ever occurring at all. What are your minimum conditions for political union? Because if you impose conditions that are too stiff, there's no point in having this discussion. You said you see all kinds of problems if you don't have political union. You've been very clear on that and convincing. But political union is not a self-defining term. Economists now find themselves drifting into political theory, but this is an important question for the monetary system. So what do you mean by political union?

Issing: I can say what it can't be. It can't be run by the Community's Commission, which is not responsible in any democratic sense. You can't still have a European Parliament that has no say on taxation. We must have a real European Parliament, and that means that the national parliament must give power to this parliament.

Cooper: Some power?

Issing: Some power.

Cooper: Not all their power? That's a question.

Issing: I see, of course, that my position may lead to the suspicion that I am imposing impossible preconditions.

Johnson: May I say that the California parliament is more powerful than many parliaments of so-called independent European governments. You don't have to give up that much power.

Cooper: Well, let's not settle this now; let's let Milton come in. But this seems to me a very important question.

Friedman: My comment is going to be directly on this point. Somehow or other, Otmar must be a very good name. At our last session in 1986, the person with whom I found myself most closely and most often in agreement was Otmar Emminger. And at this conference, the person I find myself most in agreement with is Otmar Issing. I agree with everything he said, and I want to suggest that the best discussion I know of on the problems of political union in this context was written over two hundred years ago.

Cooper: The *Federalist* papers.

Friedman: The *Federalist* paper by Alexander Hamilton. The problem of Europe is identically the problem of going from the confederacy of the states—the Articles of Confederation—to the Constitution, of going from the arrangements under which we fought the Revolution, which were showing all of the political strains thereafter. And what Alexander Hamilton said was the central element of political union was the right of the central government to have direct control of taxes over the individual citizen, without having to operate through the intermediary of the states.

Cooper: But not having exclusive control over taxes.

Friedman: No, no.

Cooper: Divided sovereignty is very important.

Friedman: Divided sovereignty is very important, but there had to be the element of direct control. I would add as an additional condition that was not relevant in Alexander Hamilton's time: a willingness to abolish all central banks. There's no other way of having an effective political union.

Solomon: Milton, everything reminds you of abolishing central banks.

Friedman: No, no, no; you can have one central bank. I mean abolishing the national central banks. I think an absolute condition of political union is that there be only one money-creating authority.

Cooper: Well, the Federal Reserve provides a model; the national central banks could be converted into district banks.

Friedman: They could be converted into district banks, but that's meaningless; the United States in effect has one central bank. Christopher thought of the possibility of Wales using devaluation against England and Scotland. And if Wales had a separate central bank, that's what would happen. It's because Britain has one central bank that you don't have that.

Now for Christopher's benefit and in line also with what Otmar was saying, I want to suggest one other reading, which is only a hundred years old and which, I think, is the best discussion of another aspect of this problem. I am referring to Bagehot's *Lombard Street*. Bagehot says that monetary arrangements cannot be created; they must grow. He was referring to the issue of free banking versus central banking, and he says that, as an abstract matter, he would prefer free banking, but by the time he was writing, the institutions had developed in such a way that free banking was no longer possible. To take a comparable example today, many people would prefer a pure gold standard, but that's no longer feasible. It might have worked a hundred years ago; it isn't going to work now.

So what I think you have to say is that it's very nice to draw these institutions on paper, to set up all of these conditions and how they're going to operate, but they aren't going to operate that way. You have forces at work, and I share very much Otmar's view that if you try to set up a central bank that is a committee of national central banks and if you try to have some kind of supranational authority that's called an independent central bank, you will find that independence is not something that's imposed from outside, it's something that evolves.

The reason why the Bundesbank has been following as successful a policy as it has is because after World War I Germany had a hyperinflation and because in 1945, 1946, and 1947 it had a period of repressed inflation, so that money no longer could serve its functions. And then you had cognac and cigarettes serve as money. France—I think this is very important—is another interesting case. The only major wars that I know of that were fought under a specie standard were the Napoleonic Wars. France never went off specie. Why not? Because a few years earlier, the French had experienced the assignat inflation. But France hasn't had a recent hyperinflation. Italy hasn't had a recent hyperinflation—big inflations, yes, but not hyperinflation.

In my opinion, Europe does not now have the political conditions for a central bank that will stick rigidly to non-inflation goals. And I don't think that this can be created simply by writing down on paper agreements among nations—nations in which there has been some surrender of national sovereignty, just as there had been some surrender of sovereignty by the American states under the Articles of Confederation. But that wasn't any good, because operations could take place only through the separate states. So I think the European case is an example of what Hayek calls "constructivism"; the Europeans are trying to construct something when they do not have the sociological, political, or economic foundation for what they are trying to construct.

Christopher said that one market requires a single currency. I don't believe that's true. I believe Otmar expressed it correctly when he said that there are two alternative circumstances under which you can have a completely integrated market. One is with completely floating exchange rates and the other is with a single currency. I believe the single currency would be an excellent institution if you could get it. But I don't believe you can get it for a Europe of many nationalities, with different languages, with different historical backgrounds, and with strong vested interests in their separate national central banks. And I believe the tendency to cite France as an example of the beneficial effects of the fixed exchange-rate discipline of the EMS is a mistake, because if you compare the non-EMS countries of the world with the EMS countries, the convergence of inflation rates among the non-EMS countries is as great as among the EMS countries. I think that France would have had a very sharp reduction of its inflation rate even if there had never been an EMS.

Rutledge: It's very puzzling to me to build an institution that is meant to be permanent, based on a situation that lasts only as long as the memory of living people. Germany has had inflations before. There is nothing I know about biology that will make the Germans have zero inflation and the French have higher tendencies, and it seems to me that if that is a large part of the reason for what the Europeans are doing, the institution is eventually doomed to fail.

Krugman: Along the same line, it's striking to me that this whole discussion is all about credibility. The traditional optimum currency arguments have disappeared completely from the discussion. Guarding against inflation is not the universal central problem of central banking; it's the problem of the 1970s and 1980s. It's not clear that this will always be the case. It was not what we would have said was the basic problem of the 1950s, let alone the 1930s. It's not a blueprint for what's going always to be the only issue for the next two generations.

I think that the case for European monetary union is by no means as clear-cut as is imagined. It really ultimately rests on the optimum-currency-area argument, and the problem with that argument is that it is very nonquantifiable, given the current state of economic knowledge. We know that an optimum currency area is more than one person and that it's less than or equal to the whole world, but we don't know quite where in the middle it is. In this connection, I'm supposed to write a report for the government of Iceland on the question of its position on the EMU. Iceland has 200,000 people. The case for participation sounds obvious, but it's not actually. You can make quite a good case either way, depending on how you feel about fish that afternoon.

Cooper: Iceland is an interesting case of a country that's had—what?—30 percent inflation, year after year, for 20 years.

Krugman: With no evident harm.

Cooper: With no evident harm.

Krugman: Right, but that's another issue. But since credibility is in fact not that important, the idea that one needs to spend a long time proving that the Europeans are really ready to have this credible central bank before they create it I don't think is right. I don't see that anything much will improve or worsen—well, a lot may worsen politically, but I don't think anything much will improve. If the Europeans decide they want a single European currency, I don't see any very strong economic argument against having it tomorrow.

Last point. Milton, if you were a European, I would not be surprised at what you said, but you're an American. We're full of institutions that were created out of thin air—created on paper but somehow becoming real. This is a country with all kinds of things that are artificial. The Federal Reserve System in the United States did not grow organically; it was just created by fiat, and suddenly there it was. And it has quite a lot of autonomy.

Friedman: I didn't tell you that you couldn't create institutions; I said monetary institutions—money, money. And Bagehot's statement was that monetary arrangements grow. The same thing is true of ours. The Federal Reserve System that was created in 1914 is not the Federal Reserve System that we have today.

Mundell: That's true.

Friedman: And it never has been what it was created to be in 1914. It has never operated the way the people who wrote that document intended it to operate. The founders established twelve Federal Reserve Banks because they thought it would be possible to have regional independence in monetary policy. And the system was created almost entirely in order to handle things like the 1907 panic.

Solomon: To provide an "elastic currency."

Cooper: To provide seasonal credit—that was the driving force.

Friedman: As for seasonal credit, it did succeed in that.

Krugman: While it may have operated very differently from the way that was intended, the creation of the system made a very great difference.

Friedman: Yes, it did; it made things worse.

Cooper: We'll discuss that tomorrow—after we adjourn!

Mundell: I like Milton's reference to Bagehot, and there's certainly some truth to it. It's not impossible to make big innovations in money, but you have to be very careful. It's safer to rely on old things that have evolved rather than on untried proposals. However, every currency that now exists was created by a sudden single act, a particular act that defined what the currency was. And the history of monetary theory and currency theory is strewn with cases of currencies that have been created and been enormously successful and cases of currencies that have been created and have failed.

Now when a currency is created within a nation state, you start off with a big advantage; you've got the power of the government. The currency is created, it's legal tender, it's got all the necessary attributes. But when you're talking about a synthetic organization of currencies in Europe, this is far more difficult because you're not sure what the political constituency is.

Paul Krugman made the observation that he was somewhat surprised that there was no discussion here of whether Europe constitutes an optimum currency area. But this is not the central issue, which is political rather than economic. If we were considering the matter only on economic grounds, I don't think we would argue that there should be a European currency. Maybe there should be a world currency. If there were an IMF currency that everybody believed in and that could be used as legal tender, perhaps most European countries would not opt for a European solution.

But the political motivation is fundamental and reflects concern about the dominant position of Germany. The motivation of the French, the Italians, and perhaps the British is based on the conviction that it will be far better to have Germany in a European system than to have Germany isolated. The political problem has, of course, been exacerbated by German unification. As the process of unification takes place, Germany will become more and more independent and may have much less interest in a European currency. But I think you all remember the circumstances that permitted the acceleration of the European currency movement. The French had worried that, as unification proceeded, the Germans would become so absorbed in German problems that they would lose interest in tying themselves to Western Europe. And Chancellor Kohl made the bargain that, in exchange for the support of the other European countries for German unification, he would support the European currency. And that's what has caused the association.

Back in 1969, I developed a plan for a European currency, and as a result of that plan the European Monetary Commission invited me in 1970 to be its consultant. I made several plans for a European currency at that time, and in the discussions that followed, a big difference emerged between what were called the economists and the monetarists. The monetarists were those people, led particularly by the French, who thought you could create a European currency quickly and then coordinate monetary policies around that single currency. And the economists said, no, you have to align interest rates, exchange rates, money supplies, budget positions, and so on, and wait until you get economic harmonization; then, at some far-off date, you can have a European currency.

Well, the people who took the latter line were, of course, the Germans. And it's quite a natural thing when you think of it. The dominant country, the big country, always has the most to lose in a monetary union for the same reason that the British in the nineteenth century resisted every effort to create a world currency. It was why the United States rejected the Keynes Plan in the 1940s, because the dollar would be an alternative to a world currency. And in the regional sphere, it's Germany that resists a European currency, because it has the most to lose. Germany has a central bank with a splendid track record that has established superb credibility.

And this is where I come to my main point. You can keep twelve central banks, you can call them regional district offices, you can give them research departments, and you can keep them nominally alive like the twelve district banks in the Federal Reserve System, but essentially you've got to have one institution. It's got to be a credible institution. And an institution in which Germany perhaps has a one-third or one-quarter voice is simply not going to be a credible institution in the framework in which it has to be created. As Otmar says, maybe in ten years, maybe after a long time period, the new institution may build up that credibility, but I think the whole opportunity will have slipped away by that time.

For that reason, I think that there's only one way for a successful European currency to be created. It can be called anything you like, but it must be based around the deutsche mark. If I were a European and were passionately devoted to the cause of a monetary union, I would go for that solution, because I think it's the only solution that will really fly. All the other solutions involve long debates and delays. I think Otmar himself so indicated; he's the economist, and the Germans will always take the view, Oh, let's harmonize, let's put it off, let's not act too quickly. So the only way you can do it is through an existing institution, and the German central bank is the only institution that could work. The Italians would go along with it, and the French would probably go along if, say, the chairman of the board were French. The governor of the Bundesbank could be president.

It's not unrealistic, if you are forming a kind of political union in Europe, to divide up the responsibilities. After all, France and Britain will certainly have the responsibility for the nuclear deterrent. And there's no reason why the Germans, who have been the most competent in the monetary sphere, shouldn't have responsibility for that. Because ultimately, in four or five years, after Germany has really digested eastern Germany, I think that the Bundestag will vote no if it comes to scrapping the deutsche mark in exchange for a European-controlled ecu.

Cooper: You spoke a long time; I'm going to ask you to speak a little more. What, exactly, does it mean to be based on the deutsche mark? You have a new European currency, but you say it has to be based on the deutsche mark. Concretely and institutionally, what does that mean?

Mundell: It means Europeanizing the Bundesbank—taking over the Bundesbank, making it a European institution.

Cooper: That means changing the statutes.

Mundell: Well, the details; let's leave those out.

Cooper: We have Otmar sitting on the board now. You're going to put Italians and French on the board.

Mundell: Let's first work out the mechanism, and then we can go to the institutional details. The new European Bundesbank takes in all the European currencies, the non-DM currencies, and replaces them with deutsche marks or with new bank notes equivalent to deutsche marks, stamped with pictures of Michelangelo or Lord Nelson or whoever are symbols of the other countries—Europeanized pieces of paper called ecus. Research people and so on from the other countries could be brought into the bank, and . . .

Rutledge [interrupting]: Ruin it.

Mundell: Not ruin it, but you would have to bring in some people from the other countries.

Friedman: Convert all the national central banks into currency boards.

Mundell: Yes.

Solomon: Just to interpret, what Bob is saying is that in the first stage all the national currencies would be exchanged for deutsche marks; the Bundesbank would be the single central monetary institution; the Bank of France and the Bank of Italy would be like the twelve Federal Reserve Banks. That's your first stage.

Mundell: Right.

Solomon: For the first five years or so. And deutsche marks would be used throughout the European Community as a currency.

Cooper: But stamped, maybe.

Solomon: Whatever—with Lord Nelson's picture. I'm just trying to understand you, as Dick was. But at some later stage, you'd stop calling it a deutsche mark and call it an ecu. Is that the Mundell Plan?

Mundell: Or, as an alternative, instead of scrapping the deutsche mark, you could introduce the ecu equal to ten deutsche marks, for example.

Cooper: But the decision making would remain for some unspecified length of time in the hands of the existing Bundesbank.

Mundell: Right.

Cooper: I think that's the key to your proposal, isn't it? The existing Bundesbank would take on the role of the European central bank under German direction. That's like Georgia and South Carolina agreeing that New York should dominate the Federal Reserve decision making.

Solomon: Can we ask our British member what he thinks of that?

Johnson: I have just one question, What would the German Länder think about it? Each German state is represented on the Bundesbank Council, and that's very important to them. It seems to me you have to have two tiers. You can't have a take-over of the Bundesbank without creating something else within Germany to be the equivalent of what the Bank of England and the Bank of France would become.

Rutledge: This is just a follow-on. How long do you believe this differential discipline is good for? I'd like to hear the British and the German view on that. We're not talking about the law of gravity; we're talking about a historical parameter that happened for reasons that aren't going to be there forever. I think you could make a case that, over a long period of time, British monetary policy has been better than German monetary policy.

Friedman: Historically, no question. Germany in 1871 went on the gold standard and the silver standard because of the success of British monetary policy in the prior 40 years. There's no question that this is why the Germans went on the gold standard. In the process, they destroyed the bimetallic standard worldwide.

Johnson: I think most European countries are convinced that price stability is a good thing. We've tried the other thing, and it doesn't work too well except in the very short run. We've had ten years of Mrs. Thatcher's independent monetary policy, and it has not delivered price stability. So now we want to try something different. I'm sure the Italians and the French feel the same, and I don't see the Germans wanting to give up on price stability.

Issing: Of course I don't want to comment on Professor Mundell's idea of extending the power of the Bundesbank. I think for political reasons that's out of the question. Nobody in Germany wants it. He said the largest country has the most to lose by giving up its currency. I don't think so.

Solomon: It has nothing to do with size.

Mundell: Well, it does have to do with size. The currency area with the largest size has the best monetary properties. More exactly, it's got the most elastic demand for money.

Issing: But of course you are right that the political surroundings have changed with German unification, and there is a lot of fear of Germany becoming a superpower. I think that's greatly exaggerated. Some people make it a test for Germany to show its European spirit by giving up the D-mark. But the question is not whether to give up the D-mark or not, but how to move from where we are to a stable European currency. When there was discussion about the Delors Report, and so on, regarding the best constitution for a European central bank, we could have sent a copy of the Bundesbank law.

Solomon: Or the Federal Reserve Act.

Friedman: No, no; the German law is better.

Issing: Actually, the draft statute of the governors of the central banks is very similar to the Bundesbank law; in some respects it's even better. But imposing it on Europe—that's another matter. It's not the same, and I fully agree with Milton that the basis for monetary policy in Germany, the real basis, was the shattering experience with two inflations in one generation. The Bundesbank law is not part of the German Constitution, and it could be changed by a majority of one vote in parliament. But although there are always some people, politicians, who criticize the course of the Bundesbank, especially when it's pursuing a restrictive policy, nobody really intends to change the law. It wouldn't receive support. But the historical background in Italy and France is different.

And that brings me to the next point. The German performance in monetary policy is not for biological reasons, and I am afraid that it might fade out. Nobody can guarantee that the policy of the Bundesbank 20 years from now will be the same. It could be worse, it could be better, but one cannot rely only on memory. When you ask younger people—my students, for example—about their reactions to German unification, they say, "So what about unification? Why? True, these people speak German. Okay, but we went to France, to Italy, to the United States—those people are our friends. We've never been to East Germany. We don't know any East Germans. They're bringing us problems." The older generation of course still has connections; that's about memory. And that's the point. All the inflation memory might one day fade out. Perhaps the Bank of England might have a better policy than the Bundesbank ten years from now. Or another central bank.

Johnson: May I just say that surely we are convinced by our own intellectual arguments of the virtues of price stability. Do we really need to have to rely on folk memory for what is supposed to be a scientific subject?

Krugman: There's a joke that I can't remember quite in the original, but it goes something like this: Heaven is an English policeman, an Italian cook, and a German central bank, and Hell is—well, you can figure it out [laughter].

Cooper: It is true that Germany has had in the last 70 years two serious inflations, although there can't be very many people around who remember the first one. It is also true that during this period, Germany, along with the United States, had unemployment rates of 25 percent, with devastating political consequences. And one of the problems I have in invoking historical memory on the question of inflation is, Why is it that German memory is focused on inflation and not on unemployment? That's a question that's not answered by invoking historical memory.

Friedman: I think it is, because the U.S. experience has been different from the German experience precisely because of the inflation.

Cooper: We didn't have the hyperinflation; that's right.

I'd like now to step out of the chair, if I might, and make a few remarks about the desirability of a common currency in Europe and about the political arrangements associated with it. My first comment is that I don't agree with Otmar Issing and Milton Friedman that you can really have a common market without a common currency. Now, as is always the case with these kinds of disagreements, they are half semantic, and it depends on what one means exactly by a common market. And of course one can deal—though less effectively—with the problem I'm about to pose, by having fixed but changeable exchange rates, as long as they're not changed too often.

The problem that I see is this—that most things consumers buy, but these days most things that businesses buy too, are not homogeneous products. They're products in which the business firms have some scope for influencing their price, so they actually have to make pricing decisions. In that sense, the competitive model of the homogeneous commodity is not applicable. The firms have to make pricing decisions, and if they are operating in a number of different markets, they've got to make pricing decisions for each of those markets. And if exchange rates are moving—I emphasize moving exchange rates between those markets—it creates havoc for their pricing decisions. They're operating in France and in Germany, let us say; they price their French consumers in French francs, and they price their German customers in German marks. And then the exchange rate, for reasons having to do with financial markets or whatever, moves between the franc and the mark. And that screws up their pricing enormously.

What do they do? Do they raise their German prices, lower their French prices, or decide on some combination of the two? If they don't, if they stick with a fixed price, which is the tendency of most such firms, then they create arbitrage possibilities for jobbers and brokers in commodities, which undermines or weakens their marketing strategy.

The practical problem that is posed for the business firm, I think, is twofold. One method of coping is to diversify across currency areas. In my example, you deal with the problem by locating partly in Germany and partly in France, thereby weakening some of the economic advantage of the Common Market because of possible losses of economies of scale. And the other thing you do is to appeal to your government for some kind of barrier to stop the "unfair competition" coming from, if you're in France, your German competitors, whose only advantage—because you're a first-rate businessman—has come from a depreciation of the mark, for reasons unrelated to your business. So I think that a genuine common market with floating exchange rates among the member is unsustainable in the long run.

And in this I think I have a fundamentally different view of the way the world works from what I understand to be Milton's view. I've emphasized nonhomogeneous products, but it's noteworthy that one of the major pressures for the European Monetary System in the European Community has come from the farming community. Farmers produce homogeneous products, and they certainly get very unhappy about a decline in the price of their goods that results from a falling exchange rate.

Solomon: Your analysis is about moving exchange rates. Can the Common Market and the EMS work with occasionally changing exchange rates?

Cooper: Well, so far they have.

Solomon: I wasn't clear what the upshot of your observation was.

Cooper: I was responding to a remark that Otmar made, and Milton agreed with, that you can have a common market with floating exchange rates. I'm saying that I don't think floating exchange rates are consistent with all the economic advantages we associate with a common market.

Friedman: But there's an alternative—hedging in the futures market.

Cooper: You can hedge a particular transaction; what you can't do is hedge your investment through the financial markets. The way you hedge your investment is to invest across currency areas. And that's what we'll see. But this destroys some of the economic benefits of having a common market if, in order to reduce uncertainty by hedging in this way, people don't invest in the lowest-cost place; you know the argument.

Friedman: You've not answered the question of whether with a common currency you would have less farmer pressure for subsidies.

Cooper: Yes, you will certainly continue to have farmer pressure for subsidies. But I'd like to come back to a question I posed earlier about the relation between the European Monetary Union and political responsibility. What is the minimal union that's required in order to have a satisfactory monetary union? I think there was general agreement— at least I didn't hear a dissent—that you need some kind of political backstopping for a common currency. It surely doesn't have to be a unitary state, such as France or Britain is today. The United States is not a unitary state, but it has been a functioning currency area for a couple of centuries.

So what are the minimal conditions? Let me suggest two possible arrangements. The first, which I can anticipate the objections to, is one in which you have a European central bank board as the decision-making authority—the analytical equivalent of our Open Market Committee—made up of sitting ministers of finance. They are politically responsible officials. They are responsible to their governments, they are answerable to their parliaments, they can be questioned, they can be thrown out—each one, one by one. This is what I would think of as minimal political accountability.

What about central bank independence? My answer to that is one that Otmar and Milton both gave this morning, which is that central bank independence lies mainly in public opinion and not in constitutional arrangements. I would argue that from a formal point of view the Federal Reserve is the most independent central bank in the world. And the reason is that we have a presidential system rather than a parliamentary system. In a parliamentary system—concretely, Germany, because much is made of the Bundesbank—if the government becomes really dissatisfied with the central bank and has the votes in parliament, it can simply change the central bank law. It's no big problem; that is routine in a parliamentary system. If the government wants to do something, it either has the votes or fails on the votes. What protects the Bundesbank is public opinion. There would be public outrage at any chancellor who attempted to change the Bundesbank in a fundamental way. So, it's not the protection of the statute; it's the protection of public opinion. The protection in this central bank board made up of sitting ministers of finance is that no single minister or small group of them would have a decisive voice. Of course, if the relevant majority of the central bank governors wanted to inflate, they would inflate. But that is true today.

Friedman: Would you require unanimity?

Cooper: I would not require unanimity, but I might require a good deal more than a simple majority.

Friedman: Then are you going to weight the vote by population or what?

Cooper: Otmar and I had an interesting discussion about that, and as I ruminated on it, I think the drift of the discussion in Europe is correct. I'm not now talking about my ministers of finance, so maybe I shouldn't shift ground, but I had always thought the vote should be weighted. Otmar tells me the discussions are drifting away from that now to individuals voting their consciences, so to speak. Each board member, whatever country he comes from, is supposed to take a European-wide view, and that idea would be compromised if in fact there were weighted votes. I see considerable merit in that.

Friedman: The Senate instead of the House.

Cooper: The Senate instead of the House, yes. So the political accountability would come through sitting ministers and the protection of the Community as a whole against short-run political pressures. This is what I think we really mean by central bank independence; we do not want governments to be able to determine monetary policy for short-run ends. Protection is in numbers, essentially—the fact that there would have to be a substantial majority of the group all in agreement to deviate from the previously agreed path.

Mundell: Would these be weighted votes?

Cooper: Well, let's leave that on the table as an issue to be resolved. The votes probably would have to be weighted if the board members were ministers of finance, but not necessarily under a different arrangement.

Johnson: What would you do with all the existing central bank governors—pension them off?

Cooper: That's a transition problem that is not of a fundamental character, it seems to me. I think a natural solution would be to have each of the national central banks be the banks of issue and be the regional arms of the central bank council, which would be the executive arm, very much as the twelve district banks were conceived to be originally in the United States and in some respects still are. The key monetary decisions are made in Washington, but the issue and distribution of currency and so forth—all that's decentralized.

Johnson: Of course, the district banks are represented on the Open Market Committee. That's the difference between your system and most of the European proposals.

Cooper: Well, I'm trying to address the minimal union required while still getting democratic political accountability. And that's the minimum I've been able to think of. You may want to go much further than that because you may be offended by the idea of having ministers of finance make monetary policy rather than independent folks—either existing central bank governors or other European citizens who are appointed for this purpose alone. But then that raises the question that Otmar raised, What about the political accountability of these people?

Johnson: They would be accountable to national parliaments, as they are now.

Cooper: They are not now accountable to national parliaments.

Johnson: Well, they have to explain what they have done. It's an ex post accountability; they don't get instructions from their governments, but they have to explain afterward to their parliaments.

Cooper: You may know more about it than I do. My impression is that the Federal Reserve System stands out in the amount of public testimony that it does, and it actually can be called before the Congress. The arrangements vary from country to country in Europe, but the governor of the Bank of England, as far as I know, is never subject to question periods.

Johnson: Oh, yes—before the Treasury Select Committee.

Cooper: Before the Select Committee, but his boss is the chancellor of the Exchequer. Alan Greenspan's boss is not the secretary of the treasury. Anyway, my other suggestion, which is much more ambitious and, I think, reflects more of the spirit of what Otmar was talking about, is to endow the European Parliament with real powers that would make the European central bank accountable to it. And although one gets into questions of judgment here, I'm inclined to agree with Milton Friedman and his reference to Alexander Hamilton that if you're going to go that route, you have to give the European Parliament taxing power to deal with the central fiscal problems of the Community, the main one of which is today the Common Agricultural Policy.

But I have another radical suggestion that is designed to deal with the Italian problem, the Irish problem, and the like, which is that there should be—again following Alexander Hamilton—a consolidation of existing governmental debt in the Community and that all of the national debt as of a certain date—let's say January 1, 1991 so as not to influence future behavior—would actually be taken over by the Community to clean the slate fiscally for the national governments as far as the past is concerned.

Johnson: The Italians would love it.

Cooper: I know the Italians would love it. I mentioned this to an Italian official, and he said, "I'll get a medal now from Secretary of the Treasury Carli for this proposal." It has the twofold advantage of putting all of the countries as of the starting date of monetary union on a fiscal par, so they don't have the inherited burden of the past to deal with. They would still have the divergencies in their current spending to deal with. The other advantage is to give Brussels a financial responsibility other than the Common Agricultural Policy. The central authority would have to tax to service the inherited debt, as well as to pay the salaries of the central institutions, and that would be in addition to the one main charge now, which is the Common Agricultural Policy.

So this would represent a partial step toward a politically united Europe that falls far short of a federation. I guess one could call it a confederation. So my question to everyone, but especially to the Europeans, is, What do you have in mind about political accountability? And are my suggestions, which are deliberately modest compared with a full federation, sufficient or do you have in mind something more ambitious than that?

Friedman: If I may interrupt to add a historical note, do you know how Alexander Hamilton achieved debt consolidation?

Cooper: Tell us.

Friedman: Well, there were two steps in it. Almost a majority of the members of the House had bought at depreciated prices the state obligations that were going to be consolidated, and Hamilton's brother-in-law hired a ship that went up and down the coast to pick up all of these obligations at ten cents on the dollar. The next step was a deal that Hamilton made with James Madison and maybe Jefferson—I'm not sure who—to have the capital shifted from Philadelphia to the District of Columbia. That provided the remaining votes needed for the debt consolidation. So it was not an easy matter.

Cooper: Like some economic models, history is overdetermined. I always thought the District of Columbia deal was made over the ending of the slave trade. That's the way I learned it. The deal that was struck was the ending of the slave trade in exchange for moving the capital south to the District of Columbia.

Friedman: No, I once wrote a *Newsweek* column on it; that's how I happened to know about it. I'll send you a copy of my *Newsweek* column.

Cooper: Well, give me your references; I'd love to see them.

Friedman: If Europeans are willing to consolidate the national debt, they'll do anything.

Issing: That would have been one of my answers. The other one is with respect to accountability. That's an issue now in Europe. It was one in Germany from time to time, and I am not happy about forms of accountability in which the monetary decision process is brought into the political scene—putting finance ministers on the board and having them not only reporting to, but being responsible to, the parliament. I think that this would change monetary policy fundamentally, bring it into the political arena, and subject it to the party in power. So with respect to accountability, you have to set a clear target for an independent central bank. And of course you need sanctions if the central bank doesn't meet this target. But if you really want the central bank to be independent, it must stick to a target that is set by the democratic process; I don't see anything undemocratic about that.

Cooper: But isn't it true—and Milton will be delighted—that if you are really to set these targets, you don't have any need for a central bank board? You just put the target into the computer. You can change the target from time to time through whatever process the European Parliament establishes. You just reprogram the computer, and you save a lot of salaries. You can go back to teaching.

Johnson: Could I just come in on this question of accountability? I think maybe Otmar and I mean different things when we use the word. A central bank can be accountable to a parliament in the sense of appearing before the appropriate committee, answering questions on what it has done and why—which is quite a different thing from having to receive orders as to how it is to fulfill its function, either from parliament or from a minister selected by that parliament. You could have the central bank governors of each country forming your European Open Market Committee, but the finance ministers could have a representative sitting there, or as in the Dutch system, the finance ministry representative might have the option of making it, as it were, an issue of confidence if he didn't like what the central bank was doing.

Cooper: That's also possible in Germany.

Johnson: Yes, I think it is. And of course the European central bank would have an obligation to maintain price stability, but also to take into account the economic policies of the European Common Market. In other words, the bank couldn't be entirely oblivious to things like unemployment and German unification. The German case is a good example of where economic policy actually overtrumped short-term monetary policy. The Bundesbank had to accept something which was suboptimal from the point of view of pure price stability. So I think you would have to have certain compromises, but you can have a machinery which gives enough autonomy to the European central bank to assure that price stability is better served than it would be by putting the objective under direct political control. It's a separation of powers, if you like—not quite on the American model, but a new European model.

Cooper: Just so I understand, you would have central bank governors accountable to national parliaments, not to the European Parliament.

Johnson: Well, they could be accountable to the European Parliament, but at this stage the European Parliament does not have, shall we say, the strong backing of national governments.

Cooper: I understand. I'm thinking ahead to the next stage.

Johnson: Well, as long as you have national parliaments and national central banks fulfilling some kind of subordinate function, there might be some kind of accountability. A national parliament would be a good forum for the European central bank to explain what it has been doing.

Let's say that once a year the governor of the European central bank appears before a select committee of each national parliament and, of course, the European Parliament.

Issing: Christopher Johnson talks about central bank governors and finance ministers, but both are appointed through the political process.

Cooper: But I consider accountability to be more directly related to removability than to the appointment process. It is true that, in the United States, members of the Federal Reserve Board of Governors are appointed by the president and confirmed by the Senate, but for a fourteen-year term. And it is remarkable how rapidly most of them lose their political coloration. The key thing is that they are not removable.

Friedman: They *don't* lose their political coloration.

Cooper: They don't lose their views of the world, but most of them lose their political coloration.

Friedman: In fact, as study after study has shown, if you want to know what the policy of the Fed is, you do better to know the name of the president than you do to know the name of the Fed chairman.

Cooper: That's a different matter; it shows that the Fed is in fact responsive to the political system as a whole—no question about that. I was talking about the individuals losing their political coloration.

Friedman: But the Fed chairman serves for a four-year term as chairman. And there has been only one case where a chairman who was not reappointed has continued on the board and that is Marriner Eccles, who remained on the board for another year until he called a press conference to announce the attempt by the president to run the Fed.

Cooper: I didn't say that presidents desisted from trying to influence the board, nor that the Fed is never influenced by the political environment—only that the individual appointees lose their political coloration.

Mundell: Eccles was demoted to vice chairman, wasn't he?

Solomon: No, he was not; he simply remained as another governor.

Cooper: He lost his chairmanship, but he had an appointment that continued.

Issing: Let me make a point about institutions. As an attempt to achieve European integration, one can imagine just having a law that decrees a free flow of goods, services, people, and capital. Then you need only a European Supreme Court and sanctions, without creating any other new institutions. And before the European Community was founded, people like Gottfried Haberler and Milton Friedman were against creating institutions. But I believe that without new institutions, we would have made far less progress toward the removal of barriers within Western Europe. So we must steer a middle course, seeking the right institutions. I think Margaret Thatcher was right in stressing the danger of having too much concentration in Europe, but to my mind, she underestimated the problem of really finding the right institutions for Europe. Of course we all know that institutions, once created, survive almost forever.

Cooper: That means you must be careful.

Issing: But new institutions are sometimes necessary. We want a stable situation—one that can survive in times of trouble.

Willett: I think all of us who are thinking about international monetary issues have a tendency to want to tinker with institutions and grand designs, but Milton and others have issued a healthy warning— that, for example, the Bundesbank's apparent independence may be due more to the particular historical situation than to the institutional design. That's a caveat that we all ought to keep in mind. On the other hand, I am inclined to think that institutions can make a difference. I have been reading a good deal of political science literature recently on international organizations, and the political scientists are having a debate very similar to the one we're having today as to whether international organizations have much influence or whether all is due to the underlying power structure and history. And they are, I think, as much up in the air on this as we are.

I do think it is important, though, for the Europeans, if they decide to move in that direction, to give a lot of thought to the design of a European central bank. There are better and worse ways of doing this in terms of independence, and I would just cite as one example the U.S. case. There have recently been a number of studies that have found that in open-market decision-making, the regional Federal Reserve presidents on average have voted for significantly more restrictive policies than has the Fed Board of Governors. This hasn't been well explained. Perhaps it is due to the less political nature of the appointments to the regional banks than of those in Washington. But it would be useful to reflect on the implications that this might have for the construction of a European central bank.

Krugman: We're being a little philosophical here, and without talking about the actual institutions that might work for Europe, it might be interesting to just step back a bit. It seems to me that there's a strong temptation to have a kind of holy trinity here—to think that one Europe, one market, one money all go together necessarily, because it's such a pretty picture, and it is essential to have each of these legs of the tripod to support the others. It's not at all clear to me that this is true. I don't think we know that, and I'd like to talk about it for a minute.

Let me offer an observation where I'm reasonably sure of my footing on the question of whether having an integrated market makes it easier to have a single money. There tends to be a presumption—as I think a lot of the EC Commission's work has suggested—that once Europe is truly integrated, then the optimum currency argument will be stronger, and it will be much more reasonable to have a single currency. This is by no means clear. It is very likely that as the European market becomes more integrated, European regions, some of which are nation-sized, will become more specialized, and the size of idiosyncratic shocks will be larger, which means that the cost of not being able to adjust the exchange rate will be greater.

Europeans, I think, have an idealized view of how the United States works as a monetary union. In fact, we're subject to enormous regional shocks. U.S. regions that are the size of European countries are substantially more specialized than European countries. It's instructive to do a comparison of the industrial structure of the South and the Midwest in the United States and compare those differences with Italy and Germany. You discover that although the South and the Midwest are much more similar culturally than are Italy and Germany, they are much more different industrially than Italy and Germany are, so the size of idiosyncratic shocks on those regions, which are country-size by European standards, are much larger. So it's not at all clear that a more integrated market for goods and services actually makes an area more suitable as a currency union.

The other issue is how much political union is needed for monetary union. I don't think we know quite how to answer that, although we have to answer it even if we don't know how. But I was thinking about a parable on how you could end up with a single currency without a political union. Imagine that Germany had never been unified, and imagine that the House of Fugger had never gone bankrupt. Suppose that, over the course of the centuries, the bank notes issued by some one private bank would have become so widely used because of their reliability and the bank's sound policies that eventually they would have come to be accepted as the medium of exchange throughout the German-speaking world. Just as the Zollverein [a custom union] happened without political union, one could imagine the bank notes of the private bank being accepted as legal tender by the German principalities—tiny Ruritanias—without a political union. The United States had a monetary union long before we had some of the things that we've said here are preconditions, such as a large federal transfer program. So it's not clear to me that these are necessary conditions at all.

Friedman: They aren't necessary conditions under some circumstances. For example, when we had a gold standard, every country accepted it, yet there was no political union among these countries. Really the most workable arrangement for Europe would be to go back to a gold standard. From the point of view of workability without political union, that would be feasible. And, indeed, if you go back in history, you had the Roman denarius, which was a silver coin that did what you're talking about; it circulated all over Europe.

Krugman [showing a credit card]: This is a pretty good international medium of exchange. It's amazingly usable.

Friedman: Yes, it is.

Frankel: Let the record show that Paul held up a Citibank card.

Friedman: The need for a transfer arrangement is not because of monetary union; it's because of the way in which the political structures have developed. As long as in the United States the central government was small and local governments were large—two-thirds of government spending was at the local and state level until 1929—we didn't have any need for a federal transfer program.

Hinshaw: I would like to dwell briefly on a successful form of European monetary union that took place in the 1950s. I served for two three-month periods as the acting U.S. deputy representative on the European Payments Union, and as everyone knows who knows about these things, the deputies, most of whom in this case were stationed in Paris, attended far more meetings on the institution's operations than the principals, who met in Paris only once a month and who, as top officials of their respective central banks, spent most of their time managing those banks. The EPU was an institution that was designed to end a terrible currency mess in Western Europe. It transformed that situation from a regime of bilateral payments agreements to immediate convertibility within the system and ultimately to convertibility with the dollar. The unit of account was not called the dollar for political reasons, but it was the dollar. Accounts were settled partly in dollars and partly in credit, and unlike most institutions, the EPU, after eight years of spectacular progress in removing restrictions on trade and payments, came to an end. It had achieved its objectives. In my view, it was a splendid example of European cooperation.

Cooper: I don't pretend to be an expert on the whole panoply of international organizations, but as far as I am aware the EPU is the only one that has ever literally gone out of existence. Some have been renamed; the League of Nations Health Office became WHO, and so forth, but I think the EPU is the only example of something that actually went out of existence.

Solomon: The only *international* institution.

Cooper: International institution, yes.

Rutledge: I'm concerned about what would happen in Paul Krugman's parable if you had this Hayekian private money around and then there were an announced change in the ownership of the bank. I think that's what you're looking at here with what you're proposing. You're trying to create an artificial situation using German discipline, with other countries not in control, and I think you finally end up debasing the currency. And the currency here is the credibility of the Bundesbank. There is now a European central bank in place, the Bundesbank. I can buy German marks any day of the week. I can write contracts in German marks if I want to. You Europeans have now at least one pure version of that thing you're trying to create, and I worry about that.

But you are not going to end up with a system where the Bundesbank controls European monetary policy; I just don't believe that. It strikes me that when you're creating institutions, you should create something that's designed to last longer than the lifetimes of the creators. And that's not what you're doing. What you're doing is taking advantage of certain behavioral properties shown by the Bundesbank in the last 20 years.

Mundell: Forty years.

Rutledge: Forty years isn't much in the length of time we should be talking about.

Johnson: I think that John has a point here. To put it quite crudely, the danger is that you end up with a majority of left-wing socialist governments in Europe and that they more or less force the central monetary institution to favor full employment over price stability. And that, indeed, is one thing that Mrs. Thatcher was worried about, although we have had examples of socialist governments behaving in a highly responsible right-wing manner, as in France, preferring price stability to full employment. So these adverse expectations may turn out not to be fulfilled.

But I think the way you deal with this problem, admitting that it is a danger, is by appointing your members of the central bank institution for longer terms than those of the governments. Those governments have terms of four or five years in Europe, and if you establish terms of ten or maybe fourteen years on the American pattern, you can give the institution a greater durability of policy than the member governments, which is why I think some of the governments are in favor of it. They are saying, Well, you know, we don't trust ourselves— even less do we trust our political opponents—to keep things going in the direction of price stability.

Frankel: I have two points. One of them is on these last comments of Christopher Johnson and John Rutledge regarding what kind of monetary institutions would be most likely to provide monetary discipline and whether independence would do that. But first I want to make another point in response to something Paul Krugman said a few minutes ago—that it's not clear that more trade, more integration of goods markets, would make it easier to have exchange-rate or monetary integration. I'm a little surprised at that. Paul mentioned earlier the optimum-currency-area literature, which traditionally says that, yes, the higher the percentage of traded goods, the easier it is, the more sensible it is, to integrate. If specialization is the result of more trade, I would think that this is clear. Now there is the question, Which should come first, goods-market integration or monetary integration? The answer is suggested by the limiting example of an individual. Those of us here are completely specialized in economics, yet it's clearly not relevant or appropriate for each of us to have our own individual money.

But on the other point regarding institutions, there's an implicit proposition that is running through what several people are saying, though I think not everyone here believes it—I think Milton Friedman does not—that if we talk about creating institutions for the future, where we don't know whether the Germans are going to be sitting on the board or whoever, does independence from the political process make it more likely that there will be low and stable monetary growth? Many of us, I think, would say that the answer is yes. Milton has often argued the reverse—that if the Fed were more directly brought under the control of the Treasury or of the Congress, made more democratic, we would get a lower and stabler money growth. I don't think that's true or a correct reading of the politics, but I think it would be good to discuss the matter explicitly, because whether accountability or independence means more stable money growth is a fundamental question about how the world works that underlies everything we're saying.

The alternative idea is that there is such a thing as a central banker culture embodied, for example, in someone like Paul Volcker, who has spent his whole life training for the job. There is clearly something of a central banker culture. But as Dick Cooper pointed out, even those who get appointed later in life rapidly seem to lose their political stripes. I can think of examples like Manuel Johnson, where it was predicted that he would be for easy money, but then, as soon as he got the job, or soon after, he adopted the central bank culture. Maybe it's just being assigned responsibility for price stability officially, or maybe it's the property of not being able to be removed by the politicians, that produces that. But when we're trying to decide what design for a European monetary system would establish monetary discipline, it seems to me that the key condition is independence.

Friedman: May I comment on that? I believe that the key consideration is how you define stability. I have no doubt that independence gives you greater stability over very short periods. My point has always been that independence is more likely to give you major disturbances—that the United States would never have had the Great Depression of the 1930s if we had not had a quasi-independent central bank. Similarly, we would not have had the great inflations that we have had. On minor fluctuations, there's no doubt that political interference will make matters worse. But if Congress hadn't listened to the Fed in 1930–31, the story would have been wholly different.

Frankel: What about the fact that in every election year, the White House and the Treasury lean on the Fed to expand?

Friedman: First of all, it's not entirely true.

Frankel: What counterexamples do you have in mind? Jimmy Carter's is the only one I can think of.

Friedman: I am not going to argue that independent central banks— real independent central banks—may not give you short-term stability. The problem is that what the central bank does in general is to allow small disturbances to grow into big ones. If the small disturbances are really random—if you've really got a random walk—it's fine. But the central bank may make a mistake and permit what it thinks is a transitory phenomenon to escalate. Central banks have great difficulty in admitting that they've made mistakes. I have read the reports to Congress, I think, of every Fed chairman for about 50 years, and Alan Greenspan has a first to his credit; he's the first chairman of the U.S. central bank who has ever said publicly in Congress, "Maybe we made a mistake." The first one! In 1931, '32, and '33, the Fed chairman who was reporting to Congress was saying that if the Fed hadn't done the right thing, the situation would have been still worse.

Frankel: What about finance ministers and senators?

Friedman: They're just as bad.

Frankel: Well, but that's the point.

Friedman: But they're subject to direct political control. They have short terms. Hoover got kicked out of office, but the chairman of the Fed didn't. The political forces are such that they prevent these small things from growing into very big ones—at least that's my interpretation of American institutions. Maybe it's different in other countries; I'm not prepared to comment on that. So far as American history is concerned, I think it's overwhelmingly clear that we have had more instability since the creation of the Federal Reserve System than we had before. If you compare the century before 1914 with the 76 years since . . .

Frankel [interrupting]: A lot of things have changed during the twentieth century.

Friedman: A lot of things have changed during the twentieth century, but I don't believe that the problems of the 1920s and 1930s can be explained by those things that have changed. And you had the same problem with central banks in Europe. Take the case of France, with an independent Bank of France, which in 1926 stabilized the exchange rate at a level that undervalued the franc. A year earlier, sterling was stabilized at an exchange rate that overvalued the pound. It was a combination of these two things that drove the pound off gold and made it possible for the Bank of France, with the help of the Fed, to suck the gold from the other central banks of Europe. These developments played a major role in creating the Great Depression.

Krugman: Why?

Friedman: Because the Bank of France, although it had no legal independence, was headed by a man who exercised personal independence, a man who told Poincaré, the prime minister, "You can fire me, but you can't make me do what I don't want to do."

Solomon: Milton, are you going to claim that if the Bank of France had not been independent, France would not have undervalued its currency? France had undervalued its currency throughout modern history. I think this has no relevance to the independence of central banks.

Friedman: No, I'm saying that if the Bank of France had not acted independently, but instead had followed Poincaré, it would not have undervalued its currency.

Willett: I don't want to challenge Milton's prewar conclusions, because I think he has an important point there. But the evidence for the postwar period seems to be pretty systematic. A number of us have done studies for the postwar years, and there we get major differences, with the institutionally dependent central banks having quite a bit higher average inflation rates. This holds up even if we take out the intermediate level of developing countries like, say, Turkey or Greece, and rely only on the major industrial countries. So at least for the postwar era, there does seem to have been a systematic difference, with the more democratically accountable central banks being responsible for a good bit higher average inflation rates.

Friedman: Well, what about stability? The issue isn't just higher inflation.

Willett: The difference holds up with stability, although not as dramatically as with average inflation rates.

Hinshaw: Milton has implied that the Federal Reserve is usually not on the side of the angels, and I would like to point out one time when I think it was very much on the angels' side. World War II was financed at a long-term interest rate of 2.5 percent, which meant that the Fed had to support this rate by buying at par all the government bonds not bought by other purchasers. The Fed went along with this policy during the war, but became increasingly restive after the war, because it regarded itself as being forced to be an engine of inflation. This was the issue over which Marriner Eccles in 1948 resigned as Fed chairman. He went to President Truman and explained his position. The president, of course, wanted to keep interest rates from rising, and Eccles said (this may not be an exact quote), "If this is your position, I will have to resign." And the president is reported to have replied, "If that's the way you feel, you should resign." Eccles was replaced as chairman by Thomas McCabe, president of the Scott Paper Company, who Truman thought would agree to keep interest rates down. But the Federal Reserve governors and staff quickly convinced the new chairman that the Fed was right and the Treasury was wrong.

Cooper: Then the president appointed William McChesney Martin, Jr., as chairman, and the story goes that he said to Martin, who had been his assistant secretary of the treasury, "Now Bill, I want you to keep interest rates down," and Martin is alleged to have said, "Mr. President, I can't promise that." And, having gone through this experience before, the president reportedly said, "Well, do the best you can."

Johnson: Perhaps I could just return to one or two questions. I think the main one that's been left hanging in the air is the optimum currency area. And I think what I would mean by this is that you move toward an optimum currency area if you are spending an increasing amount on each others' goods and services. Now Paul Krugman quite rightly corrected my formulation of this yesterday. It's not just the proportion of your GNP you do in external trade; it's that plus the proportion of your external trade you do with your partners in the optimum currency area. Now this has certainly been going up in the case of the United Kingdom. As in most countries, our imports go up faster than our GNP. We're becoming more open, and within those imports, which are now 33 percent of the GNP, well over 50 percent is done with other Common Market countries; so that's about 17 percent of total expenditure—and rising. And the smaller the country is, the higher its proportion is; which is why countries like Belgium and the Netherlands tend to be even more in favor of currency unification, because they are more optimum for a currency area than perhaps the United Kingdom is.

But the point is that this is a dynamic situation. We are seeking in a sense to make ourselves into an optimum currency area from the point of view of trade and commerce by bringing down trade barriers. And I would of course agree with the point which Dick Cooper emphasized—that it's not that you can't have a common market without a common currency; it's simply that the market will function very much more efficiently if you do have a single currency. So I think we are actually in the business of trying to make ourselves into an optimum currency area, if we are not one already.

The second point I wanted to make is about the credibility of the new monetary institution. I think the argument between the Germans and the others is that the others want the European central bank and the ecu to have a track record in preparation for making the ecu the single currency, whereas I think the Germans are saying, Well, the D-mark already has a track record; if we can make the switch from the D-mark to the ecu on Big Bang Day, then we shall be all right. And I think we're saying, Okay, the D-mark has credibility, but this thing is going to be called the ecu, and by making it a hard ecu we give it extra credibility. I don't think its credibility disappears the day you abolish national currencies, because you are actually trying to make the hard ecu into something like the D-mark. But I think it would help to have some experience in operating the new currency before we suddenly go over to it.

There's just one final point about the behavior of pay bargaining in different kinds of regimes. You can produce examples and counterexamples. There is no doubt that the German pay behavior has benefited because of the credibility of German monetary policy. And, if you like, what we're trying to do is to extend the credibility of Germany's monetary policy to other countries via the exchange rate. Clearly, the anchor has to be an existing zone of monetary stability, which has to be Germany. But insofar as we in other countries can gain credibility at the national level—which we are now trying again to do in Britain, having rather lost it in the last few years—then, clearly, wage-bargaining behavior is more likely to be favorably modified.

7.

The Issue of Regionalism

Introduced by Robert A. Mundell

Chairman Cooper: We certainly have not exhausted the topic of European currency union, but I suspect we've hit diminishing returns, and what I suggest we do now—we'll see how far we get with it—is to examine the question of regionalism, which Bob Mundell raised yesterday. Perhaps we can ask Bob to elaborate a little on his concern. For the sake of discussion, let's stipulate that the sketch that Christopher gave us this morning of the evolution of European monetary cooperation does in fact take place—that the Europeans move through stage one at least into stage two and possibly stage three by the year 2000, although we're not quite clear what that looks like. But the evolution continues. What, then, are the regional issues? Remind us, Bob, what your concerns were.

Mundell: It's hard to know where to start, but the best place is probably the European Community and especially the increase in the movement toward Western European integration, which is becoming a very expansive force, moving into the south of Europe. Who knows whether it will move into Eastern Europe? Whether indirectly or directly as a consequence of that, there has been a movement toward regionalism in North America—Canada and the United States, with perhaps the movement expanding to include Mexico. If Western Europe forms a clear-cut bloc, then this will create a tendency for a bloc to create itself in some form or other in Eastern Europe.

That's one tendency. I mentioned that certain factors, such as the decline in the Cold War, are moving in the other direction—back toward the nation state. Now another alternative to regionalism would be multilateralism. An alternative to the creation of a European currency would be the creation of an international currency. But those people in Europe who are pushing for a regional bloc won't have much interest in a global solution. And the countries that aren't part of a bloc will feel left out and will try to find some alternative arrangement, either by forming a new bloc or by joining one of the other blocs. This is the sort of trend that people have noticed, and I think it's hard to say whether it's desirable or not—whether it's permanent, whether it's basic, whether it's vital. But if a European currency proceeds as it's intended to, then this will promote much greater regional organization of the world economy.

Johnson: Perhaps I could reply to that. I think the Eastern European countries are in fact very anxious to link up with West European economic and monetary union. Now it's clear that they're not yet ready. They can't coordinate policy and inflation rates to the degree needed to qualify for membership here and now. But we're all talking about a kind of associate status which they would have. The intention would be that after perhaps ten years they would join not only the Common Market but also the common currency, because in Poland, for example, they're already conscious of the virtues of an external exchange-rate discipline, and I think they would sooner link up with the ecu than with the dollar, which they're now using as a peg. So I think you have to envisage something like, if not a 50-state, at least a 25-state European common federation with its own currency. And what I think people are talking about in the Soviet Union—those who still believe that reform might be possible—is the creation of something like the European Economic Community, in which each Soviet Republic could have its political independence but work within a Soviet common market with the ruble as a common currency.

So that in a sense takes care of about another quarter of the world. And then you have the yen and the obvious possible linkages with the other major countries in Asia. I think what you get to is that this leaves the developing countries rather out in the cold. When you look at what they do, many of them do in fact operate a currency peg. They can't maintain it all the time, but they either peg to a basket of commodities or to the dollar or to the French franc or to something—maybe a crawling peg rather than a fixed one. It seems to me that we're approaching the question of world monetary reform piecemeal, which may be the only practical way one can do it. It's better to have a common currency in one region of the world than to be too ambitious and try to have a world currency in one go—and then not have even any kind of regional arrangement to show for it.

Solomon: Perhaps I missed something that Bob Mundell said, but I had trouble understanding the reason for his forecast that some countries will feel left out. Who will feel left out and therefore feel some desire to form another regional bloc?

Cooper: Don't we have to be clear—at least I feel the need to be clear—about what regionalism means in terms of its actual content and what it means to say we have a bloc? The Canadians went to great lengths to say throughout the process of forming the U.S.-Canada free trade area that this was not in conflict with multilateralism, and I am inclined to agree with them. The U.S.-Canadian agreement took for granted the GATT system and whatever progress the GATT system could make under the Uruguay Round, but it went further in two respects. First, it went into the area of services, which was not covered by the GATT at all, and in that sense set a model for the Uruguay Round on services. And, secondly, it tacked the United States down in a way that hadn't been done before on the various procedural nontariff barriers that the United States has introduced over the last many years. On both counts, those features are consistent with multilateralism. It's true that if you view the arrangement in one way, you could call it a bloc, though I wouldn't use the term. It's certainly a manifestation of regionalism, but on the other hand, it's not regionalism as opposed to multilateralism; it's regionalism as a way station toward multilateralism.

That's one kind of thing—a completely different kind of thing from a group that decides, as in a way Britain did in 1932, that the rest of the world is too difficult to deal with. Britain formed a somewhat protective bloc within what was then called the British Empire. Then there's a third dimension here. We've been talking earlier about currency blocs, which are different from trade blocs. I haven't heard anything in the Canadian debate suggesting that Canada ought to either adopt the U.S. dollar or form a greater Federal Reserve Board. Charlie Kindleberger used to be an advocate of that, but I'm not aware that there has been anything along these lines in the Canadian discussion.

Mundell: In Mexico that issue has come up—whether there should be a North American currency bloc. But if you start to think of extending the North American free-trade area to Mexico, I think this creates a problem for the rest of Latin America. This is a big issue, as Mexico is a big country. Of course there are national-security reasons associated with wanting Mexico in this bloc—to make North America more self-contained, and so on. But whatever the basic motivation is, this is certainly going to create a new situation for Latin America.

Cooper: It creates a problem in the same sense that the formation of the Common Market created a problem for Switzerland—I mean the possibility of trade diversion.

Mundell: Yes, and when Eastern Europe forms its own bloc, that will mean a different relationship, I think, between Germany and the surrounding countries in Western Europe.

Krugman: A practical point; I think that although one may say that some kind of regional arrangement is not in conflict with multilateralism, my sense is that in practice multilaterialism is in trouble in large part because it's having trouble coping with differences in industrial structure, as between Japan and the United States. What look like trade barriers from the U.S. point of view, look like just different ways of doing business to the Japanese. And the increasing creativity of bureaucrats is making it harder and harder to police policies that distort trade. What's happening in these regional arrangements is that countries that are neighbors and have sufficiently similar systems, as well as a great deal of understanding and trust, are able basically to sacrifice a little bit of national sovereignty and establish easier ways of dealing with things that you can't deal with in GATT negotiations. And to that extent, it's at least draining energy from the multilateral process.

On another point, Christopher Johnson was talking about currency blocs as if it's better to have a few around the world than none at all. I don't know that this is true of currency blocs; it's certainly not necessarily true of trading blocs. I'd like to report an exercise using a very stylized model of the world economy, which you would imagine as being divided into some number of blocs, with each bloc pursuing an optimal tariff policy, taking the others' optimal tariff policy as given and just self-interested. You might ask, How is world welfare affected by the number of blocs into which the world is divided? You might think at first that, well, the fewer blocs the better, but actually that's not true because the market power of the blocs grows as there are fewer of them, and so they become more protectionist against one another. For all parameter values that I was able to try, the worst of all worlds is three blocs. I don't take that too seriously, but it's worth thinking about.

Johnson: Are you assuming that the blocs are common markets rather than free-trade areas? There is an important difference. In other words, do they have a common external tariff?

Krugman: That's right; they have a common external tariff.

Mundell: If I might comment, it's interesting that almost all of the conferences of the Bologna-Claremont series have been concerned with international monetary reform, whereas at this conference we haven't been talking about that but have spent a great deal of time trying to solve the problem of how Europe should create its own Western European currency. And this is an indication of the drain of effort that will occupy the attention of the Europeans maybe for the whole decade, with no energy left over to worry about international monetary reform. That raises the question of what's going to happen to the countries in Africa and Asia and South America. Who's going to play ball for them? Is that problem going to be left in the lap of the United States and Japan? Or would it turn out that if Western Europe forms its own monetary bloc, the G-7 may break down into a G-5 or a G-4 or a G-2?

Friedman: Paul Krugman mentioned the problem of trade diversion versus trade creation, which Jacob Viner emphasized in his famous book *The Customs Union Issue.* Have there been any estimates of the relative proportions of trade diversion and trade creation in the European Common Market? That is a very important consideration in answering Paul's question about trade blocs and world welfare.

Cooper: The only study I'm familiar with is a Ph.D. dissertation done at Yale in the early 1970s. I hesitate to rely on memory, but the conclusion was that the effect of the Common Market was predominantly but not exclusively trade creation. If I had to guess, I would say three quarters trade creation—three dollars of trade creation for every dollar of trade diversion in the industrial area. The study didn't take on agriculture, and agriculture, as we all know, has been a major problem in which, certainly as compared with a free-trade regime or as compared with the status quo ante, there has been an enormous amount of trade diversion. The Europeans essentially took the view: We're bound to screw up agricultural policy; let's do it on a Community-wide level. So it's conceptually hard to figure out what's going on now, but there has been an enormous amount of trade diversion compared with the status quo ante.

Friedman: We probably need a third category there, trade destruction. I want to make a comment on something Christopher said about the Eastern European countries. I don't see any reason whatsoever why the Eastern European countries cannot today link their currencies to the D-mark. In fact, I think it would be the most healthy thing they could possibly do.

Johnson: I agree that they could do this. That still doesn't mean that they're ready for integration of trade, but they could become members of the currency bloc.

Cooper: And at least in the case of Poland and Hungary, they're especially interested in agriculture—in access to the agricultural market.

Friedman: That's right. There's no question at all in my mind that if you add up the pluses and minuses in the European Common Market, the Common Agricultural Policy has to be put down as one of the very large minuses from the point of view of the world as a whole and particularly the underdeveloped countries of the world. And the United States shares, of course, in that indictment.

Let me add a sort of side point. Christopher gave me a copy of a recent book, *The Wartime Diaries of Lionel Robbins and James Meade,* and

I understandably looked in the index for Aaron Director, who is my brother-in-law and Rose's brother. There is a report in there on an evening meal that Robbins had with Aaron, and it ends with the following paragraph, which is strictly relevant to what we've been saying here. The year is 1943. Robbins writes: "We did not discuss Hot Springs. But as we were saying goodbye, he [Aaron] said to me, 'I see you're going next week to this great meeting which is going to fix the triple A (the Agricultural Adjustment Act [of 1933] on the world.'" Robbins goes on to say, "I regard this as highly significant."

Cooper: The notion of regionalism or blocs usually conjures up at least three: one centered on Europe, one centered on the United States, and one centered on Japan. We don't have here any representatives from Japan or southeast Asia, but my impression, at least at this stage (who knows what 30 years from now will bring?), is that the notion of a bloc centered on Japan is something that looks realistic only from the perspective of the Atlantic. The other Asian countries are not at all keen to link themselves in any formal way with Japan. Japan is sensitive to that and therefore not at all keen to encourage it. And, indeed, the informal official overtures that I'm aware of are between various Asian countries and the United States, not between Asian countries and Japan. So, if we think of regionalism at all, we should not fall into the habit of thinking of it as something symmetrical, with the nice three symmetrical centers of attention.

Krugman: Except that if I were going to make that case, I would say that Japan is Japan, and things don't have to be planned, they just happen. If you actually look at the surge in Japanese manufactured imports from developing countries in the last two years, they're from southeast Asia and to a large extent are products of overseas subsidiaries of Japanese multinational firms investing in southeast Asia. And I'm not sure I believe this, but you could certainly argue that Japan is forming an implicit trade bloc in the same way it has implicitly formed everything else.

Cooper: Well, then we've got to be clear, very clear, on what we mean by a bloc. If we mean thick trade relations and nothing more or thick trade relations supplemented by some foreign investment, then one can imagine this kind of evolution.

Mundell: It's a "coprosperity sphere."

Cooper: It seems to me that the policy of the United States ought to be anti-bloc. That is to say, we should be encouraging African countries to trade with North America and Japan and should wean them away from Europe because of the Big Brother phenomenon. We've got three

North-South Big Brother relationships—between the United States and the Latin American countries, between Europe and parts of Africa, and between Japan and southeast Asia. Each has its own history, much of which is at least perceived to be negative, and for that reason I think we should encourage long-distance rather than short-distance trade.

Friedman: Distance measured how?

Cooper: Geographically. Let me suggest that we move now to the subject of currency areas. Christopher suggested, on the assumption that there would be a common European currency, that it would be used extensively beyond the Common Market itself.

Johnson: Yes. I really want to pick up a point of Bob Mundell's, where he said that the formation of a European currency was distracting attention from world currency ideas. I wonder whether this is so, because it seems to me that we had the Plaza and Louvre agreements, and all this was going on while the EMS was forging ahead. One didn't seem to distract from the other. But I think we've got to ask why the Louvre agreement has sort of petered out. Is it because the dollar bounced back in 1988? Is it true that the only reason why the Louvre agreement got on the road was that the Americans really got worried about the dollar falling too sharply, so that once the heat was off the dollar, did all the steam go out of the agreement because of that? Was it also because policy coordination by the G-3 with each other seemed to be really not worth doing? I don't think it was because the EMS was developing that people lost interest in the Louvre agreement; I think there were wider reasons for that.

Krugman: The contrast between the European currency bloc idea and the U.S.-Canadian agreement raises an interesting question. If it's so terribly important to have one money if you're going to have one market, why do the Canadians have no interest in that? It is certainly not for lack of understanding; as we know, Canadians produce the best international economists. I think it just shows how much politics and intellectual fashion are dictating this, rather than any certainty about what is actually necessary.

Friedman: The reason the Louvre agreement came to an end was because Japan and Germany didn't want to accumulate any more dollars. They were stuffed to the gills with dollars, and they thought they had more than done their part.

Johnson: But I thought you said yesterday that the problem was that the United States was accumulating D-marks. That was when the Louvre agreement was falling apart; the U.S. didn't need it any longer.

Friedman: No, I don't believe that the U.S. didn't need it anymore, but I believe that a condition had been created in which it was no longer possible to prevent the dollar from falling, because the Japanese and the Germans were no longer willing to buy up dollars.

Johnson: Yes, but the reason they stopped buying dollars was that they didn't need to anymore; the dollar recovered spontaneously.

Friedman: No, no, no. If you look at the end of the Louvre agreement, that was when the dollar fell very sharply.

Mundell: Which Louvre agreement—the first or the second one?

Solomon: February of 1987.

Mundell: But then there was a second Louvre agreement.

Friedman: I see. I'm talking about the first one, and that came to an end surely because it couldn't be maintained any longer, and then the dollar fell very sharply.

Johnson: As I see it, then, the Louvre agreement . . .

Frankel [interrupting]: The first or the second?

Johnson: Well, between the first and the second, the dollar was coming down a staircase. What the first Louvre agreement did was to steady it at each step. In other words, instead of the dollar falling vertically, the agreement helped it to come down in steps.

Friedman: On the contrary, what the Louvre agreement did was to make the fall steeper than it would have been otherwise, because a private movement of capital was replaced by a government movement of capital. So the adjustment that would have occurred as a result of a gradually falling exchange rate did not take place. And when the Germans and the Japanese were no longer willing to eat dollars, you needed a larger fall in the exchange rate than otherwise would have been necessary.

Johnson: But those dollars were the best investment they ever made; the dollars went up by 20 percent in the following year.

Friedman: We would have to look at the figures. I'm not sure that's right, because they first went down sharply.

Johnson: Then they went up. It depends on the time period.

Friedman: I once estimated that it cost Japan $5 billion during 1987. When was the Louvre agreement?

Mundell: February 1987 was the first.

Friedman: I was talking about the first.

Mundell: But the second Louvre agreement was after the stock-market crash; it was in December 1987. You keep saying that the Louvre agreement broke up, but it was never abandoned. The G-7 kept paying lip service to it. But it's true that the dollar around the time of the Louvre agreement was about 160 yen, and this rate couldn't be held by the end of 1987. But then came the big turnaround when the dollar hit bottom and the Japanese held in the line at about 123 yen. I remember that very well because I wrote a newspaper article, published only in Japanese, in which I recommended that the Bank of Japan latch onto a good deal and stop the fall of the dollar by just invading the forward market. And that was discussed a lot in Japan. I don't know what happened, but I do know that the dollar rebounded sharply after that.

Solomon: I think we should attribute that to Bob Mundell.

Cooper: I wonder, Bob, if you want to rise to Paul Krugman's challenge on the question of whether a floating Canadian-U.S. dollar exchange rate is now, or is likely to become, a problem as we move through the transition to the free-trade area, which, after all, is going to take a decade.

Mundell: Yes, I'll make a comment on that. Of course there has been a difference of opinion in Canada about what monetary policy should be and what exchange-rate policy should be and about the extent to which the Bank of Canada should take account of the exchange rate. And for a new institution called the Canadian Economic Policy Review Board, these have been prime questions for discussion. The board includes about 20 economists from all over Canada, and the group more or less believes that it would be better to stabilize the Canadian dollar, but not at the present level that's been held up by the governor of the Bank of Canada.

The history of that is interesting. The new governor took office in 1987 and announced a few months later that he was going to change the historical pattern of Canadian policy and move to a zero inflation rate. And he was going to use monetary policy to do that. The Canadian dollar at that time was 71 American cents, and he allowed the Canadian dollar to go up to 87 cents. As a result of that policy, he may have stabilized, not allowing the Canadian dollar to continue to rise, but Canada now is in a recession. The big real-estate market difficulties are more severe than those in the United States. In the light of this information, a lot of Canadians think that it would be far better for Canada to have a fixed exchange rate—at a rate perhaps more like 75 cents than 85 cents.

But a more important issue within Canada comes from the confederal problem of Quebec, because Canada may be in the process of splitting apart, with Quebec going its own way. Some of the French-

Canadian economists, who have been particularly irate at the tight-money policies responsible for an especially severe recession in Quebec, think that Quebec would be better off with a separate currency area that would allow Quebec to stabilize against the U.S. dollar rather than against the Canadian dollar.

So this is a very touchy, delicate issue. I have argued for the past 30 years that Canada would be better off with a fixed exchange rate, and I'd be willing to go toward a kind of monetary union or a really fixed exchange-rate system, because in the long run Canadian monetary policy has always been worse than American monetary policy, owing to the different problems in Canada. The argument in the 1950s for going to a floating rate was so that Canada could insulate itself from the U.S. business cycle, but the Canadian business cycle mimicked the American business cycle even more severely than before, so that Canada got nothing out of the flexible exchange rate. And then when it fixed the exchange rate in the 1960s, it had a stable, much better result, perhaps one of the best results that Canada has ever had—a very good decade for Canada.

But then Canada moved back to a floating exchange rate again in 1970. The Canadian dollar appreciated in one year by about 10 percent, and that stopped the inflation. For a short time—too short—the Canadians had zero inflation, but later they kept using world inflation as an excuse for an expansionary monetary policy, and as a result the Canadian dollar, which traditionally was more or less around parity with the U.S. dollar, fell all the way down to 70 cents. And the price level in Canada was about 30 percent higher than before. So monetary policy was worse than it would have been had Canada just maintained a fixed exchange rate with the U.S. dollar.

Cooper: Anything else on regionalism? If not, let's go on to Eastern European monetary issues.

8.

Monetary Issues in Eastern Europe

Introduced by Richard N. Cooper

Chairman Cooper: Let me ask if we have any experts on Eastern Europe in this group?

Solomon: You.

Cooper: I've had some involvement over the last year. Let me perhaps begin the discussion by saying first a little bit about the situation and, secondly, what at least some of the countries face. As you all know, the Communist method of organizing an economy has now been universally recognized, even in the Soviet Union, as being bankrupt. That system focused very heavily on a physical allocation system in which prices and the monetary system played an extremely incidental role—one is tempted to say an accounting role, but it was less than that; even the accounts were messed up. And so, one by one, the emerging market economies are grappling with what kind of regime they should put in place, how exactly to do it, and how fast to do it.

The answer, I think, is fairly clear in Poland, Czechoslovakia, and Hungary, and at least arguably in Rumania and Bulgaria, though they're somewhat less clear. Basically, they want to be like Western European economies. They have a model. There's not any ambiguity in the three northern countries about where they want to be, and the only questions are the tactical ones of how to change the whole economic system—which is a nontrivial problem.

It's much more complicated in the Soviet Union, because there is as yet, as I perceive it, no consensus on where the people want to end up. There is a group of economic reformers who have the view I've just described. They want to be, as they put it, a normal economy. They want to be like a Western economy, but that is by no means a universally accepted view. So in the Soviet Union, objectives and tactical dynamics are still all mixed up, and that makes the situation especially confusing. It would be confusing enough if it were just in the economic domain, but as you all know, it involves also the question of the relationship of the union to the various republics and subrepublics and autonomous regions as well. So there's political, constitutional turmoil as well as economic turmoil.

Hungary has been engaged in economic reform for a long time—

20 years—and to oversimplify somewhat, I think it's fair to say that Hungary has followed essentially the route that the Western European countries followed in the 1950s—that is to say, it has a clear idea about the direction, moves very slowly, and then, depending on which Hungarian you talk to, some will describe the movement as imperceptibly slow while others will describe it as very impressive. But the fact is that in Hungary, while it has moved prices toward world levels and liberalized some prices, most of the prices are still controlled. Hungary does not have a convertible currency yet, but it has a moderate tariff and relatively easy licensing. But all imports are still licensed, so that the country still has a control regime not too different from some Western European countries in the early 1950s or a number of developing countries around the world. As far as I can tell, the Hungarians seem to be comfortable on that path, and so I see another ten to twenty years as they gradually become a normal economy.

Solomon: Could I add a word on Hungary? One country I have been involved with is Hungary. In addition to the problems you mentioned, many of Hungary's industries are really noneconomic. They depended upon exports to the Soviet Union, shipping goods that they couldn't have possibly sold anywhere else.

Cooper: That's true of all these countries, actually.

Solomon: They are known as loss-making industries; that's a polite term for them in Hungary. They were heavily subsidized, and I don't think the Hungarians have yet solved the problem of what to do with them.

Cooper: That problem is not peculiar to Hungary. Let me turn now to Poland, which ran into a macroeconomic crisis. Poland had a hyperinflation or very close to it. It took what is called the "big bang" approach, and on January 1, 1990, moved to a currency that was convertible on current account officially and, practically speaking, convertible on capital account as well, although technically not. The zloty was pegged to the dollar at a heavily depreciated fixed exchange rate. The Poles tightened up on monetary and fiscal policy and tried to do it all at once—all at once meaning moving to the world price structure and in the process trying to privatize enterprises as rapidly as possible. There are 8,000 enterprises that they want to privatize. They brought in some investment bankers from London to help them with this process. They should have greeted the investment bankers with more skepticism than they did. After eight months of work, the investment bankers essentially said, We can't help you because we don't have any basis for valuing the firms—which anyone who had thought about it for fifteen minutes ahead of time would have known. So the Poles have been set back in the process by, I don't know, six to nine months, but they're starting now to think about a voucher system of the type that the Czechs are about to introduce.

Czechoslovakia, as of January 1, 1991, has also gone to current-account convertibility at a fixed and unified exchange rate, rather over the reservations of the finance minister, who (I think) would have preferred a floating exchange rate. The Czechs did not have the macroeconomic problem that Poland did. They have had very tight monetary and fiscal policy during the past year, and indeed Czechoslovakia is one of only perhaps half a dozen or so countries in the world that are running good-sized budget surpluses at the present time. The Czechs have a scheme that is to be launched by April 1 to privatize the state-owned enterprises. That obviously will take some period of time, but the intention is to launch it in the spring of this year, and they may end up being ahead of Poland and indeed all of the other Eastern European countries in this regard. I should explain that the privatization problem focuses on the rather large enterprises—that in all three of these countries, as I understand it, there are now a lot of small private enterprises and service activities that have sprung up.

Mundell: Dick, how did Czechoslovakia achieve the stabilization program?

Cooper: Czechoslovakia, I'm told, has traditionally—and in this case tradition goes back to the beginning of the country in the 1920s—pursued a very conservative monetary and fiscal policy, and that tradition was not lost during the years of Communist rule. So when the new government came in, in December 1989, explicitly with a plan to change the economic system and with a fairly clear idea about what it thought was required, tightening fiscal policy just involved tightening it a couple of notches, moving from a very small budget deficit to a surplus—very unlike the Polish situation in that regard.

The Soviet Union is, one can only say, in macroeconomic chaos at the present time. The budget deficit, before allowing for the new subsidies that have just been agreed on (the difference between wholesale prices, which were freed on January 1, and retail prices, which were not freed), is estimated at 10 percent of GNP, and the current estimate—nobody really knows—is 20 percent for 1991. There are all kinds of proposals for what to do about the currency. You are all aware—I know nothing more about it than what I read in the paper— that there was a partial currency reform last week in the sense of declaring that, three days after the announcement, all 50-ruble and

100-ruble notes would cease to be currency. This is really a capital levy on at least the large holders of these particular notes. That's by way of general background.

There will be a lot of debate about whether what Poland and Czechoslovakia did is correct, and there will be a lot of ex post analysis. For Poland, 1990 was a rough year. Output, as officially measured, fell very sharply. The rate of inflation also fell very sharply, but not as much as had been hoped, by the end of the year. The two positive elements are that reserves grew enormously and the country ran a foreign-trade surplus for the first time in a long time. That partly reflected the decline in economic activity. But, as one Polish official put it to me, *homo economicus* is certainly not dead in Poland. One can see incipient entrepreneurship all over the place, and that's a very positive sign.

Well, just to make a point on statistics—since Lionel and Milton raised the subject earlier—Poland is especially a case where we cannot take the official indices at face value. Take, for instance, the decline in real wages—that is, the decline in money wages divided by the official price index, a price index that reflected, I won't say nothing real, but very little real, because you couldn't buy goods at the old prices. So the question is what it means to have a consumer-price index that is made up of goods that you can't buy at those prices. But the scope of goods (especially) and services that people can buy has been greatly widened by virtues of opening the country to foreign trade. So the decline in real wages is real if you understand what the indices are, but it is certainly not a measure of welfare.

Johnson: When you measure nominal zloty wages against the dollar, they've gone up quite sharply.

Cooper: Because the Polish real exchange rate, adjusted for inflation, has appreciated.

Friedman: The Poles grossly undervalued the zloty, and gradually that undervaluation has been declining. That's why you get the sharp rise in Polish nominal wages when measured in dollars.

Cooper: Well, just to finish my remarks on Eastern Europe, some Poles are now having second thoughts about what they've done, but as far as the other countries are concerned, what kind of monetary regime they should have is still an open matter. There's a very lively debate in the Soviet Union over a parallel currency, which Milton suggested; over going to a currency board; over dollarization—just allowing dollars to circulate as a medium; over a major currency reform à la Germany in 1948, which the demonetization of 50-ruble and 100-ruble notes might be regarded as a step toward; or actually trying to make the existing ruble convertible. And it has to be understood that the Soviet Union is way behind Western European countries in the early 1950s. The ruble is not convertible internally. A lot of rubles that are held by enterprises can only be used for selected purposes. So internal convertibility is a step that the Russian economists certainly recognize has to come before, or be simultaneous with, the movement to external convertibility.

Friedman: As it happens, in September Rose and I spent a couple of weeks in Czechoslovakia, Hungary, and Poland. I didn't get much out of Hungary, but I did talk to various people in Czechoslovakia and Poland. We were really there for filming a documentary, not as economists, but we managed to combine the two. And what struck me— what I came away with that I hadn't realized before—is that when you say their goal is a Western economic system, that's not a self-evident term. It has two very different meanings. And I think what's really going on in both Poland and Czechoslovakia—I don't know about Hungary—is a very strong dispute between these two separate meanings.

One meaning is a Western European economic system of a welfare-state kind à la Sweden. The other is a Western European system à la Hong Kong or nineteenth-century Britain or nineteenth-century United States—a sort of real libertarian free-market alternative. In Czechoslovakia the finance minister is really a proponent of the Hong Kong arrangement. He feels very strongly—we talked to him at some length—that he has great opposition on the other side. He talked about who his opposition in parliament was to the scheme of vouchers, and he said that a considerable part comes from the people who were associated with the Dubcek experiment back in 1968. Some of them went out of the country and came back in after having made a career outside; they had been exiled—professors and so on. Some of them remained inside. They are all persuaded that the Dubcek program would have worked if the Russians hadn't stepped in. And they would just simply like to recreate that.

In Czechoslovakia we spent a day or so at the Prague School of Economics. The people there were very nice, able, decent individuals, but they don't really believe in markets. They believe in a Lange-Lerner socialist economy. I think that's where the real fight is—not only in Czechoslovakia—and in my opinion, it will make an enormous difference which of these two views prevails. Czechoslovakia is the best off of these Eastern European countries, but I don't believe that even it is rich enough to afford a Western European welfare-state economy. If it tries to do that, I think it's going to end up as a Latin American economy rather than as what it could have been.

Now in Poland we had an experience that I recorded in the *Wall Street Journal*, which brings out very sharply the difference between these two views. I met one morning with a group of legislators in the parliament who were fundamentally Hong Kong free-marketers, libertarians. This was a very nice, casual, harmonious meeting. They were interested in finding out what that involved. The next evening I gave a talk before Club Europa, which is a group of intellectuals—primarily now Solidarity intellectuals—and this one was under the auspices of the U.S. Information Agency, so I chose as my topic, "Why the U.S. is Not the Right Model for Czechoslovakia." Well, Rose and I were both brought back to comparable sessions we had in the 1960s in this country. It was a predominantly hostile audience, and they were hostile because they were in favor of government intervention and a centrally directed economy; they were just anti-Communist. Now I won't say 100 percent of them had this perspective; there were a few exceptions, but most of them remained socialist intellectuals, which they had always been. And, as you know, that was the main dividing point in the presidential election that followed. As it happened, the evening I gave my talk, some of the leaders weren't there because that was the evening on which they were holding a meeting with the primate of Poland, or whatever he was called, to decide whether the president should resign and there should be a presidential election. And much to my surprise, I found that the free-market economists I came across in Poland were all in favor of Walesa. The socialist intellectuals were all in favor of Mazowiecki.

I think this is a very real conflict. I also happened to see the new ambassador to Poland. He had a lunch for us in which he got together a lot of the government officials. The finance minister is obviously a very competent person who is in the middle of this; he is really a technician. On the other hand, next to me was sitting the man who was head of the central bank, and he was a straight Communist—no question about it. He did not have the slightest interest in establishing a free market. Across the table from me was the minister of industry, who came from the Krakow industrial group that were all for a free market. But there were people in the cabinet—most of them, I would say, from what I heard—who really did not want to privatize. If you say that privatizing was held back because of this group of advisers from England, I can't believe that. Privatization did not proceed because the people in power did not really want to privatize; they wanted to hold on to their positions. I think they've wasted a great fraction of that balance-of-payments surplus in continuing to subsidize. The reason they have had a good fiscal policy is because they had an undervalued exchange rate. As a result, they had a large inflow of funds, but instead of using that to promote investment and privatization, they really used it, as I understand it, to subsidize the continued losses of the major state enterprises.

The real hope in a country like Poland, the real hope in a country like Czechoslovakia, in my opinion, is not what the government does or does not do about privatization, but what Dick Cooper was talking about—that *homo economicus* is not dead. You can see all over Poland the real emergence of private enterprise, and the most important thing, in my opinion, that these governments could do would be simply to say that entry into any occupation or pursuit is not forbidden. Then they would have to privatize: competition would sooner or later destroy the major public enterprises. How are you going to privatize the Gdansk shipyards? How are you going to privatize Nova Huta? It's inconceivable. You can privatize a large number of the small enterprises. The small shops and so on are being privatized, though even here there are problems. When we were in Krakow, I talked to some people who were very knowledgeable, and there was a big argument about how they were going to handle the disposal of the shops and buildings owned by the city government, because much of this small property is property of the city government as opposed to the state.

McKenzie: Mrs. Thatcher privatized enterprises in Britain.

Friedman: Oh, but Mrs. Thatcher in ten years privatized only 5 percent of the economy, and those were simply mostly converted from public monopolies to private monopolies. That is not a viable pattern for Czechoslovakia and Poland. The interesting thing about this discussion in Krakow was that various alternatives were proposed. One was an auction for straight cash. Among others were auctions allowing mortgages. And who were the strongest for straight cash auctions?

Cooper: The former Communist officials—the managers.

Friedman: Sure, because they had the money. There's altogether too much talk about these people all being oriented to the free market. In many cases, markets mean altogether different things, and there are very strong movements in all of these countries for socialist markets. Now I didn't see enough of Hungary, but we met a group of Americans who were there to advise Hungary, and boy, with friends like that, Hungary doesn't need any enemies.

Cooper: Well, I understand what you're saying. I consider the Hong Kong model to represent a small minority in these countries. It happens to include Vaclav Klaus, who is the fellow in charge of economic policy in Czechoslovakia, so there's a good deal of tension there between Klaus, who is a very strong free-marketeer, and many of his fellow economists whom I would not describe as socialists, actually.

Friedman: I would.

Cooper: I know you would. But you'd describe me as a socialist, probably—anyone to the left of you. They're certainly to the left of you, but I wouldn't describe them as socialists. And I said advisedly a Western European economy, not the United States, because they're very strong on the safety-net features, and so forth. It's an interesting question you raise about whether, in fact, they can afford that. But Klaus is absolutely clear as a free-marketeer, and there is no ambiguity in his mind about it. I'm not sure that he would accept Hong Kong as a model for Czechoslovakia, but he'd snuggle up to it as closely as possible.

Friedman: Well, in Poland you have the Krakow Industrial Society, which on the whole is very much along that line. Now they are a minority; there's no question that they're a minority. But that doesn't mean that they're without influence and without some effect. I share your general appraisal, but I am pessimistic. I am afraid that the socialist marketeers are likely to come out on top, and the only way I can see of avoiding that is very rapid action.

Cooper: And that's Klaus's strategy.

Friedman: That's what Walesa is hoping to do. I'm not at all optimistic that it will work. But don't misunderstand me.

Mundell: I want to say something about this, under the heading of the bureaucracy problem. Reuven Brenner of McGill University has studied this in great detail. An example might be the Soviet Union. The Soviet Union has 18 million bureaucrats. Multiply that by three to get the number of people in the associated families, and you have almost 60 million people with a big stake in the system—in the bureaucracy with its perquisites and all those things.

So the question is, What do you do, what does Gorbachev do, to placate these people? They're in power; he can't kill them as Stalin killed off the kulaks. But that is a very real problem. The question is whether you really have to pay them off in some way or whether you have to somehow find another solution. I think that even if Gorbachev and Yeltsin do what they want to do, they will have to cope with this problem, which is rife through all the Eastern European countries.

The other thing I wanted to say is about the stabilization problem, the macroeconomic problem. There really are, as everybody here knows, about three routes you can take in this stabilization process.

One is the Polish route, which is to revalue and to let prices go up in order to get rid of the currency overhang if that is the problem. That has the defect that it penalizes the people who have saved over the period, and it also distorts relationships among generations that have saved in different proportions. Another method is currency confiscation or currency reform. Rudiger Dornbusch emphasizes this because he thinks that it follows the route that Germany followed in 1948, and will prevent people in the new world from being unequal. The difficulty with this is again age and distribution problems; some people's life savings are wiped out, so it's not fair. The third route is to link up the privatization problem with the stabilization problem and just sell off as many state assets as you need to in order to gobble up the excess currency. And that seems to me to make the ruble convertible into acres of land or into apartments or into whatever is necessary to achieve the result. This is a route that would finesse the problem.

Now I know there are many difficulties associated with that—difficulties I won't go into. At a meeting in Rome three or four weeks ago, the president of Gosbank and some minister from the Soviet Union were present, and we had long chats about these problems. Every time we made a suggestion for a solution, the president would say that it couldn't be done. So I ended up saying, "Well then, it seems to me that you're just at an optimum right now, because everything else is worse." Then he said, "No, it's impossible, we have to move, we have to move."

Johnson: I wonder if I could try to make a distinction—it may not be a distinction to Milton, but I think it should be made—and that is between the concept of the social market economy and market socialism. In Western Europe, we think what we have is a Ludwig Erhard type of social market economy, where the main means of production are in private hands, but we have a welfare-state safety net for health, education, and unemployment. Now I think that some of the people Milton calls socialists in Eastern Europe may in fact want that kind of economy rather than what I call market socialism, which means just taking the socialist structure, with all the bureaucrats still running the main firms, and trying to operate them in some kind of a market.

I think what we've discovered in the last couple of years is that market socialism doesn't work, partly because the people and the structure are wrong and partly because you can't go halfway toward having a market. What creates a market is having private traders; it's having a private distribution system as well as a mainly private production system. State-controlled companies simply do not respond to market incentives in the way that they would if they were in private hands. That is because of what's sometimes called the "soft-budget" constraint; if the bureaucrats make a loss, they know that the state will pay in order to keep them and their employees in jobs, because the alternative is too expensive—you'd be paying people to do nothing instead of paying them to at least pretend to do something. You know the old gag, "We pretend to work, and you pretend to pay us." But this system has at least produced a certain rudimentary level of goods in the Soviet economy until now.

I think privatization is the key to this. You can only move from a sort of failed market socialism to a proper market economy if you privatize the firms. We have what's called the agency problem: How do the shareholders make the firms, make the managers of those firms, act efficiently? Well, it has to be done by competition, by the threat of takeover—all these things which more or less work. Sometimes they don't work too well in our economies, but they're better than the alternative, which is simply to have the state as the major shareholder. That really never seems to work terribly well in making the managers behave in an efficient and market-like way. And I suppose the only thing we can do—we can't kill off the bureaucrats; we can't retire them all, that would be too expensive—we somehow have to retrain them to behave like managers in a capitalist system. I think that is the contribution the West could make. But it's going to be in fact a most difficult thing to do; and it can't be done overnight.

Friedman: I don't disagree with your distinction between the social market economy and market socialism. What I was saying is that I think the kind of social market economy that Western Europe mostly now has and that the United States has—in which you socialize the fruits of production instead of the means of production—is only feasible when you reach a certain level of wealth, and these countries are too poor to be able to achieve that. The second thing is that I couldn't agree with you more about privatization. When I was asked in Eastern Europe what it is that they should do, I said I have three words: privatization, privatization, and privatization! That's the key to it. Unless you can privatize, and privatize as rapidly as possible, you're in trouble. So I don't disagree with you at all on that, but I just don't think that this social market *Wirtschaft* is a real feasible possibility in Eastern Europe.

Johnson: Well, I would say it's feasible if they can be content with a much lower safety net, a lower level of welfare, than we have. They can't expect Western standards of welfare, but they can expect a bare minimum—they have been getting a bare minimum—in terms of education and health. But not in unemployment pay—that's the thing that's changing now.

McKenzie: I want to ask Milton why privatization in Poland is so extremely difficult. You certainly don't want to kill the bureaucrats who are working for these enterprises. But isn't the main thing that the enterprises should be under private ownership and that people should be able to fire the bureaucrats if they're not performing?

Friedman: Absolutely. But the bureaucrats don't like the idea.

McKenzie: Well, it's at least a lot better than other alternatives, and they might well continue in their jobs if they're people of some intelligence.

Friedman: I don't disagree with you on that. But you have to make distinctions between the kinds of companies. For outfits like Nova Huta, which is a very big, very inefficient steel plant near Krakow and a disaster in every respect you can think of—the pollution is just unbelievable—the only thing you can do is to bulldoze it. Yet it employs a very large number of people and has a lot of vested interests associated with it; the community around it depends on it. So it's extremely hard to privatize an outfit like that because it's so hopeless from an economic point of view. On the other hand, there are lots of other kinds of enterprises for which what you say is right, and it is feasible to privatize them. But there are also very strong vested interests of the kind that Bob Mundell talked about, who much prefer the present system. And the populace at large is not very happy about the idea of converting their former bureaucratic managers into wealthy stockholders.

McKenzie: Well, I can see the objections on the basis of equity, but, you know, it might actually work.

Friedman: It might work; oh, yes, I agree. I kept saying, "You must privatize."

McKenzie: Right.

Krugman: "Property is theft," but we'd rather that it be not quite that obvious.

Cooper: "Property is theft" is the old Communist line. There may be some ambiguity about the term *bureaucrat*. You both have been talking about the employees and managers of enterprises, but remember that there is a whole set of subministries. The allocational system has been a physical allocational system, so you have a lot of people who are bureaucrats in the Western sense. They're not just state employees of enterprises, but they are actually bureaucrats who can pass some paper, put their stamp on the documents, and so forth—layers of those things—for whom a genuinely new role has to be found. What is really lacking is a wholesale industry, and in a market system these bureaucrats will have to go into the wholesale trade.

Rutledge: Regarding what Milton was saying, taking over a company that produces nothing of value and selling it to someone doesn't do any good to anyone unless the buyer can then extract the resources and build all over again into something useful.

Cooper: Yes, but there is a theorem that says that every country has a comparative advantage in something. The theorem actually applies to Communist or ex-Communist countries as well as to Western countries, so that, at some exchange rate, some of those firms are going to be profitable at the world price structure, even though they may be terribly inefficient and may have terrible externalities. It should be added that in former East Germany, for example, the industries are going to have to come up to EC rules. That's a process that could be spread over a number of years. Some of the enterprises will have to be closed; at the moment, we don't know which are which.

Rutledge: I don't mean that. I mean the resources are organized the wrong way. That's the problem I see there; it's that these aren't efficient organizations for combining resources to produce things of value—not that steel or shipping or whatever are industries that aren't going to survive because they're not viable businesses. But the resources would be viable in many cases if you took them out and combined them with labor in different ways. We've gone through that here in the 1980s. We restructured a great deal of American industry—not losing jobs, not losing capital goods or anything, but just recombining resources in ways that produced more value.

Cooper: I am going to change the subject, and I'd now like the group to think about the following issue. We're supposed to be specialists in the area of monetary economics, and here we have a case where important countries are rethinking their monetary systems from scratch. Industrial countries that have not had a monetary system at all are having to face this choice. Some of them have made it, but exactly what kind of monetary system to install is not against a tabula rasa; they start with different actual situations. But, at least as a thought experiment, we can play God and tell them what kind of monetary system they ought to have, given the initial conditions. Milton, if you don't mind, would you start the discussion?

Friedman: Well, let me begin with the solution that most people now think is so good, like the Polish solution of pegging to a European currency.

Cooper: Keeping their old currency.

Friedman: Keeping their old curency, but pegging it to the mark or the dollar or whatever. If you can do that, fine. It works like a charm as long as you undervalue the currency. But now Poland has an inflation rate that is higher than the inflation rate in Germany, and the undervalued currency is shortly going to be an overvalued currency. At that point the Poles will use up their reserves, then they will devalue, and then they will go through the same process again. And that seems to me to be the reason why this solution, which seems so attractive and so desirable, may not, in fact, be the best prescription for these countries.

It seems to me that there are only two other solutions that are really desirable and satisfactory. One is to unify your currency with a foreign currency. Unify it—not peg it—the way in which the Hong Kong currency is unified with the U.S. dollar. This is the British system, an ancient one, nothing new; it's the currency-board system in which a country can create currency. Anybody in that country can create currency by depositing foreign currency; if you deposit, say, one dollar and two marks, you get back one new zloty or one new ruble or whatever you want to call it. That has the great advantage that it preserves the national currency unit and in addition enables a country to get the seigniorage on the money that it creates.

There is no reason why the new money can't be a parallel currency at a floating exchange rate with the other currency. As long as the exchange rate is floating, the currencies can circulate together. But the new currency will impose a discipline on what the government does with its own currency. If the government inflates too much, its local currency will be driven out of existence and the new currency will take over. In some ways, this solution seems to me to offer the best of both worlds.

The only other satisfactory alternative that I see is to have a local currency like the zloty with a completely floating exchange rate. If the country manages its domestic financial policy in such a way that the exchange rate is relatively stable, so much the better. If it can't, at least it doesn't have these periodic devaluations. Now there really aren't any other alternatives in the world; you either have an independent currency at a floating rate or you have an independent currency at a pegged rate or you have a unified currency. And you either have just one currency or you have several; the notion that you can't have several currencies at the same time is wrong. For example, the United States during the greenback period of the Civil War had two currencies that were circulating simultaneously: gold and greenbacks. Banks had deposits in both currencies.

Mundell: And Confederate notes.

Friedman: And Confederate notes. That was in the South; they didn't circulate very much in the North! In the North you could have gold accounts or you could have greenback accounts. In day-to-day circulation in the West—in California—gold was used as a medium of circulation. In the East greenbacks were used. The only way the government entered in was that it required customs duties to be paid in gold.

So there's no reason why you can't have parallel currencies circulating side by side. Fascinatingly enough, in the Russian hyperinflation after World War I, there existed some old tsarist currencies. Of course there was no tsar. There was nobody printing more tsarist currency, so the supply was fixed. And it appreciated very sharply. During the whole of that period, it maintained its value relative to the new Russian currency being issued by the bolsheviks. But that was a case of parallel currencies of a very different kind.

Solomon: Isn't that like cigarettes in Germany after World War II?

Friedman: Yes, that's right—cigarettes and cognac. Don't forget the cognac; that was a very important reserve. It's the most liquid currency that you can use! But sure, the benefits of having a medium of circulation are so great that people will resort to a silly thing like cigarettes if there's no other medium available, but there's no need to resort to cigarettes. Marks are much better; why not use a sensible thing like that? But I don't see that there are any other alternatives than the three I have described.

Johnson: Well, I'd like to name one which is very widely used, and that is the crawling peg. It has, in fact, been used with some success. In Brazil one can argue about how successful it was in the end, but for certain periods it was used with success. And it is, of course, being used in Mexico at the moment. The Mexicans simply preannounce what the rate of devaluation of the peso is, and they make it equal to the expected inflation differential between Mexico and the United States. I forget the exact figure, but it's of the order of difference of 20 percent a year, and therefore they say that the peso will be devalued by a tenth of a cent a day or whatever it is; it's quite a finely tuned system. But Mexico is a major commercial country, it has adapted to the system, and clearly the object is that the peg should stop crawling and settle down to a fixed peg. I think the system is quite a good one and one which would work for Poland today. It would avoid the danger that these new Polish export industries are priced out of the market by an inflation rate which is very low by Polish standards but is still higher than Western European inflation rates.

Friedman: That is a sort of variant of the pegged exchange rate. You are absolutely right that it should be included. It was used quite successful by Chile for several years, until Chile made the great mistake in 1978 of pegging to the dollar. The episodes that are fascinating from a monetary point of view are the behaviors of Chile and Israel. Chile pegged to the dollar in 1978, and it worked like a charm until 1981, when the dollar started to appreciate. Then it was a disaster. The finance minister who was responsible for the policy was kicked out of office, and the thing was changed. Israel, at the outset of its attempt to eliminate inflation in 1985, pegged to the dollar just before the dollar started to depreciate. It was a great success, and the person who put that into effect was a hero. This, implicitly, is a way of commenting on your crawling peg. I think the crawling peg is a variant of the fixed peg that is feasible at times, but I don't believe that it's really feasible in the long run because, sooner or later, those in charge are going to make a mistake about how much they should crawl.

Arndt: Back for a second to Milton's point on pegging the exchange rate. It's correct, of course, that if you peg your currency, let's say to the mark, and then you run your monetary policy at a rate that is widely inconsistent with what's happening in Germany, you're going to have to devalue. But I want to draw your attention to the Austrian example. The Austrians pegged successfully for years to the mark through their hard-currency policy; they actually agreed to let their monetary policy be driven by the German monetary policy. So you need to make a commitment that goes well beyond just fixing the exchange rate.

Friedman: You have a similar phenomenon in Panama, which uses the dollar but calls it something else.

Johnson: The balboa.

Friedman: The balboa is just the dollar. That's exactly what the Austrians have done, except they have their own currency.

Johnson: No, the difference is that the balboa is not actually used at all in Panama; it's a purely theoretical currency to keep the shreds of national sovereignty.

Mundell: The balboa *is* used. In 1903 Panama and the United States had a treaty in which the Panamanians declared they would never create a paper currency. So they created a metallic currency, which is the balboa. In fact, because there's an open casino market, you need the balboas for the slot machines. But the paper currency is all dollars.

Friedman: The Hong Kong dollar is a viable circulating currency.

Johnson: Oh, yes.

Friedman: It's unified with the U.S. dollar and essentially is the dollar.

Mundell: I like Milton's suggestion of the currency-board system as a policy, and I also agree with him that the problem with fixed exchange-rate systems that don't have tradition behind them is that they're not really credible because a new government may come in and decide to devalue. If you can take away from a government the right to devalue—perhaps though a currency-board arrangement that contains a provision that the currency can never be devalued—then this would be a good system. And that's the way in which a country like Poland could get the monetary policy of its neighbor, Germany. Now Milton said that this was an advantage over using the D-mark directly, because you can get seigniorage from it. But Poland somehow has to start out with enough reserves.

Friedman: No, no; anybody can create it. Any foreign investor who wants to come into Poland will create new zlotys. He uses these zlotys in his business, and he creates them by going to the institution, which has its headquarters in Switzerland and a board of directors consisting, say, of three Poles and three Swedes, and he deposits there the relevant dollars and marks. He receives a package of zlotys that are backed by 100 percent reserves.

Mundell: Yes, but is this behind just the marginal increments in the paper money?

Friedman: This is a new zloty—starting out from scratch.

Mundell: But let's say that we start out with the existing zlotys.

Friedman: No, no; I'm going to have those float. This is going to be a parallel currency, and the old zlotys are going to float against this new zloty. And the new zloty is going to be 100 percent backed.

Cooper: I think the point is that this particular currency either has to be earned through running a current-account surplus in order to get the foreign exchange to create the currency, or it has to be borrowed from foreigners who have the foreign currency, or Poles have to sell an asset to foreigners to get the foreign currency. In all of these three cases there are real resource transfers involved, and in that respect the new currency differs from a genuine fiat money. One could imagine—

maybe Bob was coming to this—a fiduciary tranche followed by 100 percent reserve backing.

Friedman: You could do that. But if you try to use the mark directly . . .

Cooper [interrupting]: Then you lose the seigniorage.

Friedman: And you have exactly the same problems.

Cooper: Exactly. You have that real resource problem, and you lose the seigniorage.

Mundell: The point is that the seigniorage is the interest rate on outstanding official reserves, and you can acquire that if you hold, not completely liquid assets, but assets that earn a return. You can't earn on the whole amount because you probably have to keep a part of your portfolio in really liquid assets and the rest in interest-bearing assets, as India did. India kept its reserve assets in England earning a return. So that would be gold-standard principles operating and, I think, would be a very viable system for some of the Eastern European countries. The question would be if they could, without going through another currency conversion, just take their existing assets, find the right exchange rate that makes real wage rates at about the correct level, then borrow the foreign-exchange assets. Let's say that Poland needs 10 percent of its GNP in the form of this high-powered money. Then Poland could borrow that amount from Germany, invest it in interest-bearing assets, and use the interest to repay the loan from Germany. It would be a wash; there would be no seigniorage, but the loan would provide the backing for stabilizing the currency.

Friedman: Well, what would they do internally? In order for them to do that internally, they would have to have a fiscal policy in which the difference between expenditures and receipts can be borrowed in the domestic market or in the foreign market.

Mundell: No, I'm just talking about the monetary system.

Friedman: Yes, but the monetary system cannot be separated from the fiscal situation, because in all of the cases the real reason why they have great difficulty in having stable prices is that the government is spending too damned much relative to its income.

Mundell: I know, but under any system, they're going to have to achieve fiscal discipline. So, from the standpoint of having confidence in the currency, and following up on the currency-board system for each of these countries, the prescription would be to borrow the appropriate amount for backing the existing money and to choose the right exchange rate.

Friedman: And eliminate the power of the central bank to create any more money except by this device.

Mundell: Except by an export surplus.

Friedman: Except by 100 percent backing. Incidentally, if any of you have looked at the U.S. currency figures for the last year, you will have noted that as of December 1989, when the Berlin Wall fell, the currency proceeded to take off and go for a joy ride. I've estimated that in the year since then, something like $16–20 billion of currency has been exported, to be used as money in Eastern Europe, in Argentina, in Brazil, and so on. And we're getting the seigniorage on that. We in the United States have borrowed at zero interest rates $18 billion from these poor sucker countries.

Rutledge: There's another case that may involve setting up a new monetary standard, and that is Kuwait. A massive amount of rebuilding is going to be taking place in Kuwait in the near future, and when that happens all the institutional operating systems are going to be reexamined. The exchange rate historically has been set every afternoon, based on a secret formula involving several other currencies and gold. There's an opportunity there to bring some advice to bear on how you would re-create the exchange-rate system in this very peculiar economy with essentially one revenue source—oil.

Mundell: Kuwait had a very efficient monetary system, and the Kuwaiti dinar has been one of the best of all the currencies in the Middle East. So the Kuwaitis don't really need external advice; they just need to redo what they were doing before, because they had something very close to a fully backed system. The Kuwaiti pound started off at parity with the British pound, but it hasn't depreciated like the British pound.

Friedman: Well, let me emphasize that. I don't think most of these countries need external advice. The external advice they get does them more harm than good because it's such a mixture and they have no basis for knowing whom to take seriously. I've been very impressed with their home-grown knowledge and expertise. The problem in these countries is not that they don't know what to do; the problem is getting the political backing for what really needs to be done. And I think when we go over there and try to tell them how to run their countries, we ought to come home and take care of our own countries first.

Mundell: I want to say something about this plan that Milton has outlined for Poland. To me it is a really superb way for Eastern European countries to go. And yet one has to ask why countries haven't done this before. The technology is not completely new. In Latin America they've listened to me, they've listened to Milton and to other people. Last April we had a conference on these things in Berlin, and someone from Argentina was there. He said that the Argentine cabinet had thought of using the dollar in Argentina just a few years ago because they had tried all the other measures without success. The cabinet apparently discussed the matter for hours until someone said, "But if we did this, doesn't that mean that we could no longer finance the budget by creating money?" The answer was yes, so the plan collapsed. They didn't want to be left in a position where they didn't have this option for balancing the budget.

If you lock a country into this system and the country, for good or bad reasons, has difficulty balancing the budget and does not have access to the capital market, you put the country in a position where the government is bankrupt. There would be discipline, but the discipline is bankruptcy. And if the choice is between bankruptcy and devaluation, people will always choose devaluation. I think that is the basic problem.

Cooper: But you pose the choice in stark terms. Isn't it the case in general—assuming that the world system is continuing to function—that any country on the currency-board basis could in fact go to the international capital market in any given year. I'm not talking about year after year after year in large percentages of the GNP; I'm talking about a country in any given year, if it had an earthquake or a shortfall of revenue.

Mundell: It's a problem that people are concerned about very much in discussions of the European currency plans, particularly in the case of a country like Italy, because you suddenly shift over to a European currency while Italy has a budget deficit of 10 percent of GNP. People worry about the threat of bankruptcy, given this budget deficit.

Friedman: I completely agree with you. I just think you cannot treat the monetary problem without also treating the fiscal problem. They've got to be treated together.

Cooper: So we've identified several monetary schemes. One is simply to go to a foreign currency. That has the disadvantage that you have to earn it or borrow it or sell assets. And you lose the seigniorage.

Friedman: And you also have the political disadvantage—that somehow or other it demeans a nation to use a foreign currency.

Cooper: The symbolic aspect.

Friedman: Symbolic. And that's not unimportant.

Cooper: Another possibility is the currency-board solution, in which you have to earn the foreign currency or borrow it, but you retain the seigniorage and you retain this symbolic aspect. A third possibility is what we've called the Polish solution, which is to try to make your own fiat money by having a shock treatment of some kind—an undervalued currency or an appropriately valued currency.

Now there are two other possibilities that I'd like to mention. Classifications are always arbitrary, and one can consider them in-between cases. One of them we've actually seen in the Soviet Union, which is to try to give credibility to existing currency by taking some of it away—a sort of halfway currency reform. It would be useful to register the views on that as a solution to the so-called overhang problem. I say "so-called" because, in fact, the ratio of financial assets to income in the Soviet Union is not exceptionally high; on the contrary, it's exceptionally low by Western standards. So if you look at it from a Western point of view and just look at the aggregate figures, there doesn't seem to be a currency overhang.

Another proposal is one that has been made seriously in the Soviet Union: a currency-board system without the currency board—that is to say, you have a new bank of issue that issues fiat money, but it cannot issue it to the government. It is a truly independent bank of issue, and the government cannot force it to issue money. This is, as far as I can tell, a modern version of the real bills doctrine—the issue of currency against good solid trade credit or claims. That proposal has not only been put forward by some Russian economists, but as I understand it, it is the most serious leading contender at the present time.

As I see it, apart from the points that we've talked about, seigniorage and the real resources involved, there is also the issue of credibility in all of these. The question you have to ask in the Soviet Union today or in Argentina in 1986 is, Will the public believe in a currency created by a new bank of issue that is under statutory instructions not to lend to the government, but only to issue currency against, say, some useful trade transactions? Will that make the currency a sound one? I would pose the same question with respect to a currency board. Is it really credible in an Argentina of 1986 or a Soviet Union of today for the government to set up a Hong Kong–type currency board with the face of the national heroes on the bills, and so forth, and say, Here's the way we're doing it now; please accept this in payment for your wages, and don't spend it within the next half hour. That's the issue of credibility. It seems to me that the strong case for going to a foreign currency is when confidence in the government has become so weak that the only thing that's believable is something that the government can't put its hands on at all.

Friedman: That's why I described this institution as being located in Switzerland and governed by a board on which at least half were non-Polish or non-Russian citizens.

Cooper: Yes, but you're out there in Sverdlovsk, and you're told that. Do you believe it? Here it is—a note with a hammer and sickle on it. Put a Swiss flag on it; maybe that would help do it.

Friedman: Well, suppose it happens. Only a little bit of the new currency will come in to begin with, because it's only going to come in from the sources you mentioned.

Cooper: Right.

Friedman: So the quantity will be limited. It will gradually, only gradually, grow.

Cooper: It has to build its reputation.

Friedman: Absolutely. Everything does. Incidentally, I cannot believe that it is proper to describe what Gorbachev has just done as a monetary reform.

Cooper: No, it's not; I said it's a sort of half reform.

Friedman: It's not even a half reform. The only justification I can see for it is what the *Wall Street Journal* attributed to it; he wants to incite an insurrection. It's utterly ineffective. As I see it, what you're doing is making sure that you have a higher inflation rate than you had before. Why in the world are people going to hold on to any rubles once they see that holding on to rubles is not a way to have any wealth? The government is making rubles useless.

Cooper: That's the problem with any capital levy.

Friedman: But it's worse than a capital levy in this case; it's really worse than a uniform capital levy.

Cooper: It's a capital levy on a particular class of assets, and it increases public distrust in that class of assets. I think it's a misguided solution to the so-called overhang problem, which, I think, would not be a problem if the budget were under control.

Friedman: There is no overhang; there's only repressed inflation.

Mundell: But that's what is meant by the overhang: an excess supply of currency that has its counterpart in the repressed inflation. I have some figures on this that were prepared by the Gosbank. To give a rough order of magnitude, let's say that GNP is 1 trillion rubles and the money supply is 500 billion rubles.

Friedman: Does that include deposits?

Mundell: That includes deposits—all bank deposits. This would give you an income velocity of something like 2. Now let's suppose that the equilibrium value of the money supply is 350 billion rubles. In that case, the overhang—the excess liquidity in the economy—would be 150 billion rubles. Another figure that's interesting is the total value of Soviet assets. The estimate of the head of research of the Gosbank is something like 3 trillion rubles.

Cooper: This is real assets now—capital stock?

Mundell: Yes, real assets—land and other assets. Don't ask me exactly what things that encompasses, but it is about three times GNP. Thus, if these figures are roughly correct, the monetary overhang is about 5 percent of the value of Soviet assets. This means that by selling off, by privatizing, 5 percent of the assets—what Maggie Thatcher did, though she took a long time to do it—the Soviet Union could get rid of the overhang without an inflation and without having to choose whom to reward and whom not to reward in the system.

The next thing, of course, is to introduce the currency-board system. We probably shouldn't call it that because it's got colonial attachments, but it should be accompanied by a fixed exchange rate and backed by 100 percent reserves. Jude Wanniski has proposed that Soviet gold reserves be used for this purpose, with the ruble convertible into gold. He thinks that if this proposal were put into effect and made credible, it would eat up a lot of the excess supply of rubles.

One question in this connection is how much gold the U.S.S.R. owns. I asked the research chief of the Gosbank about this, and he said, "Well, you're not going to believe me, but I don't know and the Gosbank president doesn't know. Perhaps two or three people know how much there is." But the figure is probably less than 70 million ounces—about $35 billion. Well, if you mortgaged that gold to acquire the external reserves, and made it credible, you might be able to do without a system that had 100 percent reserves, because the larger the country, the more chance there is to take advantage of insurance principles. So a country the size of the Soviet Union, by first of all utilizing the gold assets and getting a stabilization loan from the IMF, then perhaps getting handouts from Germany, Japan, and maybe the United States, would be able to have a stable currency system, a stable ruble.

But there's another issue that we've already talked about. It would be a great waste to go through all the effort to achieve a stable currency if you're not going to have the microeconomic reforms that are going to give you the output response, the supply-side response, that you need in order to win the economic game. You'll never be able to achieve the internal reform without a stable currency. On the other hand, a stable currency by itself is only part of the total picture.

Johnson: Bob, I just have one question on that. I appreciate what you say about selling 5 percent of the assets, but wouldn't it be simpler just to issue treasury bonds and mop up 150 billion rubles in that way? That was being talked about when I was in the Soviet Union.

Rutledge: Nobody will buy them; they tried that.

Mundell: Another proposal was to issue gold-backed bonds. But there's a question of whether that's really credible.

Johnson: Yes, but surely from the Russian citizens' point of view, it's better to have bonds which might pay, let's say, 15 percent interest than bank deposits which only pay 2 or 3 percent. Faced with the choice, they'd rather have bonds, wouldn't they?

Mundell: Well, what I'm suggesting is that they take the excess money that they have and trade that in for apartments or land or . . .

Johnson [interrupting]: Yes, sure, but that is politically, as you know, a much more radical step.

Mundell: But I don't see why, since everybody's talking about privatization. We're not talking about the whole thing; we're talking about 5 percent. This is not a really radical step, given what they at least say they want.

Cooper: Housing comes to mind.

Johnson: Yes, I was just about to say that.

Cooper: The problem is that with rents so low—and rents include utilities and so forth—why should anyone buy an apartment? So they've got to get the rents way up before there's an incentive. They have tried to sell bonds; there's always a question of the interest rate. They priced them at what they thought was an attractive interest rate, but the bonds didn't sell very well, so they went to lottery bonds, which attracted more buyers, and to commodity bonds that promised you, say, a refrigerator in three years, reflecting the shortage of goods there. The commodity bonds have done reasonably well, I'm told.

Mundell: I went through this apartment question. As you pointed out, rents are so low that people wouldn't want to buy the apartments. So I asked the officials, "Why don't you raise the rents?" They said that this was one of the political difficulties; there is such an excess demand for apartments that people have been waiting for years to get them and those about to get them—as well as those already in them— would be horrified by the rent rise, since they would obviously regard it as a big cut in their real wages. So I said, "Well why don't you raise rents, raise apartment prices, and raise salaries to compensate for that?" And they said, "If we do that in this case, we'll have to do it all across the board and create chaos throughout."

Friedman: You don't have to go to Russia to find this problem; you can go to New York City, where they have rent control.

Cooper: Well, maybe we've exhausted this topic for the time being, but it will be with us for the next year or two, at least.

Friedman: You're an optimist if you think it will be only for a year or two!

Cooper: Conrad Jamison wants to have a word.

Jamison: A couple of minutes. There is one area in the world that may not have been given sufficient attention at this conference, and that is the Middle East. A little has been said about that but not very much, and it seems to me that the current war in that region has unleashed or inflamed forces whose ultimate course no one can predict with assurance, except that they will be far-reaching. There will be great changes regardless of whether the war proves to be short or long, whether Israel is drawn into the fray, whether Saddam Hussein lives or dies, and whether Iraq survives as a separate nation. Regardless of any destruction that may take place in the oil facilities of the Middle East and whether OPEC hangs together or falls apart, there are still going to be vast changes. Of course, this situation may simmer down after the war is over, without many problems—and some people think that. But I still think that we ought to recognize that the war may cause a lot of change in the mechanisms we're talking about.

Cooper: Certainly, dramatic events have taken place with lots of implications, many of which are not foreseeable. I guess the question for us would be whether we can foresee any significant impact on international financial arrangements, or to put it another way, is the existing set of international financial arrangements resilient enough to absorb all kinds of shocks, including this particular one? I guess my offhand reaction would be that while these events are very dramatic, they are not likely to have a consequential impact on international financial arrangements.

9.

Economic Science Grapples with Dilemmas of International Finance

Paul A. Samuelson

When you give a named lecture, you fall into a standard pattern. For five or ten minutes you describe how distinguished the departed scholar was, how he was virtually a Renaissance man, and how honored you are to speak in his name. Then you settle into the substantive business of the evening and describe the latest findings in the domain of quaternions or *Drosophila* fruit flies.

Well, Lionel Robbins truly was a Renaissance man. Besides being economic theorist, historian of economic doctrines, exponent of pro-capitalistic policies and attitudes, and circus manager of the great pre-war zoo of LSE whiz-kids in economic science, Lord Robbins was peer of the realm, chairman of the *Financial Times*, board member of Covent Garden, the Tate, and the National Gallery, and architect of higher education reform in Britain. And he was a character in his own right. In particular, Robbins was an important player in the game our Bologna-Claremont conferences are dedicated to, the study of how international economic affairs ought to be conducted.

Therefore, I should alter the stereotyped pattern. After recalling good stories about Robbins, I can still keep him present in my various comments on what economic science can teach us about proper commercial policies and institutional reforms.

Lionel was a tall, handsome, and impressive presence. Once during a polished Robbins lecture at Harvard, a young Bob Solow whispered in my ear, "People who don't lecture like that should be shot."

Tjalling Koopmans agreed with James Mill that people should not write too well. As Koopmans put it, "One's ideas should go only so far as their merit takes them." Well, in a profession where the crime of good writing is not widespread, Robbins produced gem after gem. The finest, of course, is his youthful 1932 book, *The Nature and Significance of Economic Science*. It said what needed saying: Factual knowledge cannot yield you ethical norms. Never mind that young Lionel swallowed much Austrian guff about a priori truths and the unimportance of mea-

This chapter was originally presented as the Second Robbins Memorial Lecture.

suring quantitative relationships. It is an author's "goods," not his "bads," that survive the Darwinian gauntlet of science!

Readers of Edmund Gosse's *Father and Son* will relish Robbins's more gentle ordeal arising from being born to a fundamentalist Baptist family. I refer you to his 1971 *Autobiography of an Economist*, which like most memoirs begins better than it ends. Let me give a personal anecdote, slightly doctored, to help make the point about his ascension to the elite of the British class system. Back in Marshall Plan days, Robbins was in Paris for an inflation commission. I encountered him at an economists' cocktail party, and encounter is the right word. In cutaway garb, he looked more distinguished than any person could possibly be. Stimulated by his polite and flattering interest, I became more and more animated—until, in a crescendo of hyperventilated brilliance, I spilled all of my dry martini over his beautiful tailoring. Guilt-stricken, I proffered wrinkled kleenex to stop up the flood. Lionel turned not one hair. "Think nothing of it, my dear Paul. Have no concern."

What could I say? As an amateur anthropologist, I opined to Robbins, "On the plane from Boston to Paris, a colonial from the fringe of the British Empire moved from passenger to passenger to convey his unease concerning missing his further connection in Paris. His nervousness quite annoyed more than fifty people. And here you, Lionel, have put me completely at ease despite my gaucherie. There is really something to the British Empire Builder and his phlegm." Lionel gently punctured my pretentious balloon, saying, "Yes, Paul, that good public school I never went to did wonders for me."

I ration myself to only two more Robbins anecdotes. In 1948–49, those experts in trade theory who were not busily engaged in refuting my factor-price equalization theorem were busily engaged in proving it. When I dined as Robbins's guest at the Reform Club, he struck his forehead and said, "You know, I believe that Abba Lerner wrote a paper for my seminar on that topic back in 1933. Better still, I think I can find it in my files." He could and he did. The rest is history—Robert K. Merton history-of-science history. Abba Lerner had completely forgotten it; Joan Robinson had completely forgotten that a criticism she made of my 1948 paper was one she had already made to Abba on his 1933 paper.

The story is important to illustrate what Robbins too little emphasized in his autobiography—namely, his role in spotting and encouraging such talents as R.G.D. Allen, Abba Lerner, John and Ursula Hicks, Nicholas Kaldor, Tibor Scitovsky, Frank Hahn, Will Baumol, and many others.

The last story was told to me by Carl Kaysen, who visited LSE while on leave from the Harvard faculty. An eminent establishment figure said at a dinner party, "The Bank of England grossly mishandled the 1930–33 credit policy. You and I, Lionel, told them to expand more but they just wouldn't listen." As bystander, Kaysen reported, "In case you never heard an academic admit to error, Robbins replied, 'Give yourself all the credit you like, but count me out. I was a crazy Hayekian deflationist at that time.'"

Now I shift quickly into the substance of trade policy. In those same 1930–33 years, the young Robbins clashed with the famous Keynes over Keynes's depression abandonment of free trade. Robbins never regretted that stand on principle. As I review the debate, both antagonists had a point. Keynes did not advocate tariffs to reduce British imports; he wanted tariffs so that the United Kingdom could stimulate GNP by expansionary domestic measures and accompany the same total of imports by a full-employment economy. Once the pound fell off gold parity, Keynes got his heart's desire. And recent econometricians have confirmed Seymour Harris's study of the 1931 sterling depreciation; it did not act as a "beggar-my-neighbor" measure to rob others of jobs, but served to permit macro expansion enough to keep the Sterling Bloc good economic neighbors.

Counsel for Robbins can argue that it may be better to stand up for the shibboleth of free trade in season and out of season, lest the few departures from it that could help welfare be swamped in the long run by the many departures that entail deadweight loss.

Let me move on to consider what features of recent international finance have proved to be surprising. I always tell my students, "Study your surprises. Always look back; you may learn something from your mistakes." What would Robbins have expected in 1975–91 that the facts betrayed? I made my little list and then asked a number of experts to nominate surprises. There was surprising agreement.

1. Most experts think the volatility of floating exchange rates exceeds that which they expected.

2. My rereading of the late 1970s literature turned up virtually no predictions that America would shift massively into debtor status with chronic balance-of-payment deficits on current account. If I showed Lionel the 1960–1980 export and import totals, he could never have extrapolated the 1982–1990 gigantic sea change in their difference.

3. Even Harry Johnson, not long dead, must be astonished in Valhalla that real exchange rates have moved almost fully in step with nominal exchange rates. Johnson's simplest paradigms assumed that

differential changes in regional money stocks induced nominal exchange rates that left real exchange rates relatively invariant. That seems to be precisely what has not happened.

4. What did experts expect about elasticity optimism and elasticity pessimism? And what did the 1980s teach us on these matters? Robbins, as an eclectic to the right of center, would put considerable faith in elasticity optimism. He could be forgiven for being puzzled by the amplitude of induced terms-of-trade shifts in the post–Bretton Woods epoch of floating exchange-rates.

5. The purchasing-power-parity doctrine (PPP), which was good enough for David Ricardo and Gustav Cassel, however tempting it might seem to Robbins the antiquarian, would have been bloody expensive to the speculator in foreign exchange who listened to the version of PPP espoused by Professor McKinnon of Stanford and by the London branch of Goldman Sachs. As the pragmatist Charles S. Peirce almost said, the test of truth of your scientific hypotheses is writ large in your IRS tax return, Schedule D, of capital gains and losses.

6. America has for half a century been a low-tariff economy. The free-trade ideologues, whom Jacob Viner used to despair, aver that free trade helps everyone everywhere and at all times. That is bad Ricardian economics. Sophisticated analysts know to predict that superior technological progress by Japan and Germany in those goods in which America used to have Ricardian comparative advantage will lower U.S. real incomes and lower America's consumers' surplus from international trade. (See Straffa's *Ricardo*, 1:140–41, for Ricardo's recognition that a large improvement in England's productivity in wine would hurt Portugal absolutely.) Therefore a Lionel Robbins brought back to earth as Rip Van Winkle ought to have been unsurprised by the relative stagnation in the 1970s and 1980s of American manufacturing real wages.

7. The 1980s taught the trade experts what they had forgotten to emphasize. Domestic capital formation in America will be crowded out if low private thriftiness and nonlaughable Laffer full-employment budget deficits suck resources into producing incremental consumption goods. However, when more copious saving persists abroad in Europe and the Pacific Basin, the U.S. consumption goods splurged on can be produced abroad in extraordinary measure—so that the crowding out of our capital formation can be ameliorated or even avoided. *The resulting massive structural current-account deficit in the balance of payments is thus understood in terms of differential regional net savings rates.* And the sea-change transition from America as the largest creditor nation to America as the ever-larger largest debtor nation is seen to be in accordance with economic science and not a continuing mystery.

Tautologies do not need to be admitted, even though they do insist on being respected. But the interregional tautology that America's net investment must be matched by her net saving minus her current-account deficit does not tell us whether this takes place at yesterday's 133 yen to the dollar or at Dr. McKinnon's 199 yen to the dollar, or whether it takes place at 1980's real terms of trade or at 1991's altered terms.

8. How do I know what experts expected on New Year's Day, 1980? The then current literature is fairly fresh in my memory. Best of all, I have an infallible method for finding where the jackass of science is to be found. Like the old farmer, I say to myself, "If I were a jackass, where would I go?" And going there, I usually find the animal.

So I examine my 1972 New York speech to the Swedish-American Chamber of Commerce, entitled "International Trade for a Rich Nation." If you lack an ancient pedigree, you must forge and fabricate new traditions. When the parvenu Nobel Award in economics was created, the Federation of Swedish Industries tried to launch the idea of a little Nobel lecture, in which pearls of more popular exposition on a current topic were to be cast before a business and bureaucrat audience. When my time came, that December week in Stockholm was an over-busy one, and I had to decline the invitation. But, as it turned out, if Mohammed would not go to the mountain, the mountain would come to Mohammed. It was arranged that my discourse could be delivered later in New York before the joint Swedish-American Chamber of Commerce. What does the anthropologist practicing content analysis find in that speech? In retrospect, I have to deem it one of my better days. Here were some of the home run hits.

A. I correctly perceived how overvalued the dollar had been in the 1959–71 period and the likelihood that it would float downward in the years to come.

B. I correctly attributed this trend to the differential superiority in manufacturing productivity abroad in the Pacific Basin and the Common Market as compared with North America.

C. I correctly spotted and extrapolated a trend toward erosion of some of America's consumers' surplus from trade, as innovation abroad proliferated in industries where previously we had enjoyed comparative advantage.

I desist from further blowing of my own horn. In hindsight, what did I miss?

While I correctly extrapolated what Kravis and Lipsey have since documented—the shift of our multinationals to maintain their world share by out-sourcing their production—back in 1972 I worried about whether America's great accumulation of creditor ownership abroad would put her at political risk of not receiving her contractual principals and incomes. In short, I completely failed to foresee the 1980's falloff in American thriftiness relative to thriftiness abroad and our resulting shift to debtor status. It was as if I had anticipated the Shakespeare play but had left out the character of Juliet.

Why feel bad, you may say, for not being clairvoyant? A scientist is not supposed to be a soothsayer. There are some things one ought not to be able to predict. (The 1939–59 reversal of the long-time decline in the net reproduction rate is a good example.) Who in 1972 could have predicted the 1981 Reaganomics, in which the successful attempt to limit the growth of public expenditure by the device of reducing tax receipts would entail an important shortfall of revenues behind expenditures and an important increment in the fraction of net national product devoted to private-plus-public consumption? No one. (Indeed, many still fail to understand the Greek scenario involving this "tapeworm-therapy.")

What I do consider a proper matter of self-reproach is my lack of 1972 recognition that our best theory of overall saving behavior—that of my neighbor Franco Modigliani, based on life-cycle processes—would expect our society's reduced rates of demographic and productivity growth to lead to a lowered private saving rate in the 1980s. And maybe I should have been more alert sociologically to the erosions of modernism and affluence as they sap the bourgeois ethic and undermine both thriftiness and social altruism.

The sun is down, and time is short. In hit-and-run staccato, here are my own glosses on the eight aspects of science surprise.

1. How much is much exchange-rate instability? When Abraham Lincoln was asked how long a man's legs should be, he said, "Long enough to reach the ground." When asked what stock prices would do, Baron Rothschild said, "They'll fluctuate." When the late Henry Wallich asked me at the Fed whether I didn't agree that the dollar undergoes St. Vitus's dance, my frank answer was the Cole Porter one. Soybeans do it. The Dow Jones does it. Safe treasury bonds do it. Why won't all God's children in the organized-market zoo do it—namely, oscillate—so that, in retrospect, economists will say the movement was excessive? Am I endorsing or impugning macro-efficiency of organized markets? Not if my lawyer did his job in auditing my wordings.

2. Ex ante ain't ex post. When economic science looks back on the sea change to debtor status, an orthodox Ricardo-Dornbusch-Fischer model can model the gross facts.

In 1964 I shocked my venerable teacher, Gottfried Haberler. I said that comparative advantage theory tells us nothing about what the capital-movements components in the payments balance would be. Yes, a nation can even be undersold *in everything* without contradicting equilibrium. (Proof by enumeration: Contemplate a nation of playboys who inherited rich fathers.) Put the current deficits into the Ricardo et al. model, and it becomes neutral on whether the reduced-form exchange rates were appropriate to the reduced-form capital movements.

3, 4, 5. I must diagnose the severe swings in real exchange rates as endogenously induced and not as exogenous quasi–random walks. This must send Johnson and McKinnon back to the PPP drawing boards. It must cast doubt on extreme elasticity optimism in the effective Marshall-Lerner sense. But of similar importance, it casts doubt on Ohlin balanced-income-elasticities optimism in the transfer-of-capital context. The late Frank Graham would be pained by the cheekiness of modern facts. *C'est le guerre! C'est le science!*

Purchasing power parity of Ricardo, Cassel, and Viner began, not as a theory of one price via arbitrage, but rather as the irreducible long-run germ of truth in the quantity theory of prices. Under strong and unrealistic caveats about invariant real propensities and homogeneities, correct PPP applies to nontradables as well as tradables. Kravis, Summers, and Heston have documented that the dollar-rupee exchange rate stays in equilibrium when Professor Cassel as tourist can live at "one-third cheapness" on his diet of lentils and saris.

Science seeks precision where it can be found. Science must also seek to define imprecisions, both imprecisions in our knowledge and imprecisions that exist in the facts themselves. What the exchange rate will be must depend on what our net foreign investment will be. I wrote *our* foreign investment, but it is not something determined by us. Nor do the animal spirits of foreigners determine it. We, they, and the play of comparative advantage all interact in a kettle of chaotic processes—and I may be using the adjective in its Lorenz-Poincaré modern sense. No wonder I am wary of contemporary mixed economies making firm commitments concerning inflexible exchange rates. No wonder I am skeptical about confident forecasts of future exchange rates and balances.

6. and 8. When we go back with Haim Barkai [1990] and reexamine Britain's tragedy in the 1925 restoration of pre-1914 gold parity, we realize that from 1870 to 1914 (and again after 1918) the United States was doing to the United Kingdom what Japan has been doing to the United States in 1955–91. Even if the United Kingdom had not spent her overseas wealth in 1914–18, by 1925 the U.K. welfare state had lost much

comparative advantage. The clock should have been rewound at a lower pound parity—particularly if the United Kingdom expected to pay for her imports by new export successes.

Granted that dynamic shifts in comparative advantage can hurt a nation's welfare, can tariffs and quotas reverse this? Or are they cases where we react to a cold breeze from abroad by shooting our own feet? For a small region, there is a presumption that protectionism is self-defeating and unproductive. For a nation with more than a fifth of global output, the issue is more complex. One suspects that politics will not find the existent second-best.

7. Herman Kahn used to ask us to think the unthinkable. Years ago I made a two-society Ramsey model in which a perpetual-lived Crusoe traded with a perpetual-lived Friday, and in which Friday's rate of time-preference was biased above Crusoe's. The result was perpetually increasing indebtedness. I buried the results in a lead safe and vowed never to think of it again. Lately, I've felt some need to dig it up. Enough said.

Those who have kept awake will have spotted my game. I have an arsenal of economic tools. After being confronted with each new fact, I dig out one that fits the specimen in retrospect.

Do I remind you of someone in the following tale? A rival to William Shakespeare discovered that Will had a portable word processor. Every word of his work and the works of Lord Oxford came out of that word processor. So, in the dead of night, our aspirant to fame kidnapped from Shakespeare's house that magic word processor.

Everyone lived happily ever after. William S. reverted to his old goose quill. And all his rival had to do was to work out the software program that would bring out the words of his perfect new plays.

So it is in economic theory. We have models aplenty and can devise new ones ad hoc. All we need is the judgment and creative spark to put them together in reproduction of what it is that is out there staring at us. If we cannot stay ahead of the game, we must try not to fall too far behind.

Name Index

Allais, Maurice, 2
Allen, R. G. D., 150
Arndt, Sven W., 79, 138

Bagehot, Walter, 87, 89–90
Barkai, Haim, 155
Baumol, William, 150
Brenner, Reuven, 131
Brittan, Sam, 82
Bush, George, 31

Cassel, Gustav, 152, 155
Cooper, Richard N., 2–3, 5, 11–15, 17, 21–29, 31, 34–37, 39, 47–48, 50–51, 54, 58–61, 63, 65, 68–73, 75, 79, 81–83, 85–93, 95–100, 101–4, 107, 109, 111–12, 114–16, 118–20, 122–28, 130–31, 134–35, 139–40, 142–47
Cowperthwaite, Sir John, 22

Denison, Edward, 15
Director, Aaron, 119
Dornbusch, Rudiger W., 132, 154
Douglas, Paul H., 15, 34

Eccles, Marriner S., 103, 111
Emminger, Otmar, 86
Erhard, Ludwig, 132

Fleming, Marcus, 44
Frankel, Jeffrey A., 11, 14, 17–18, 24, 44, 54–55, 56, 61–65, 67, 74, 106, 108–10, 121
Friedman, Milton, 2, 4–10, 13–17, 19–20, 22, 24–29, 33, 35, 38, 49–54, 59–62, 64–72, 86–90, 93–98, 100–101, 103, 106, 108–11, 118–21, 127–42, 144, 147

Friedman, Rose, 49, 119, 128–29

Gorbachev, Mikhail, 131, 144
Gosse, Edmund, 150
Graham, Frank D., 155
Greenspan, Alan, 25, 100

Haberler, Gottfried, 104, 155
Hahn, Frank, 150
Hamilton, Alexander, 86, 100–101
Harris, Seymour E., 151
Hayek, Friedrich, 88
Hicks, Sir John, 150
Hicks, Ursula, 150
Hinshaw, Randall, 1–5, 10, 33, 68, 106, 111
Honecker, Erich, 55
Hoover, Herbert, 110
Hussein, Saddam, 147

Issing, Otmar, 8, 20, 37–42, 46–49, 53, 55, 57, 59–60, 63, 65, 74, 83–88, 91–92, 100–101, 103–4

Jamison, Conrad C., 4, 85, 147
Jefferson, Thomas, 101
Johnson, Christopher, 8, 18–19, 22, 29, 31, 44–45, 50–51, 57–58, 65, 75–83, 85–87, 93–95, 99–103, 107–8, 111–13, 115, 117–18, 120–21, 127, 132–34, 137–39, 146
Johnson, Harry G., 151
Johnson, Manuel H., 109

Kahn, Herman, 156
Kaldor, Nicholas, 150
Kaysen, Carl, 151

157

Keynes, John Maynard, 11
Kindleberger, Charles P., 116
Klaus, Vaclav, 131
Kohl, Helmut, 8, 55, 91
Koopmans, Tjalling, 149
Kravis, Irving B., 153
Krugman, Paul R., 3, 10–11, 15–18, 20–
    22, 27–28, 33–35, 42–43, 48, 50–51, 54–
    58, 61, 65–67, 69, 72, 88–90, 104–8,
    112, 116–20, 134

Laffer, Arthur B., 31, 54, 152
Lerner, Abba P., 150
Lucas, Robert, 51, 53

McCabe, Thomas B., 111
McKenzie, Lionel W., 20–21, 127, 130,
    134
McKinnon, Ronald I., 152–53, 155
Madison, James, 101
Martin, William McChesney, Jr., 111
Meade, James, 118
Merton, Robert K., 150
Mill, James, 149
Modigliani, Franco, 154
Moynihan, Daniel P., 34
Mundell, Robert A., 3, 5–7, 10, 12, 17,
    21, 26–27, 30–33, 35–36, 43–45, 50–54,
    56–57, 62, 67–69, 71, 75, 80–82, 89–94,
    99, 103, 107, 114–23, 126, 131–32, 138–
    42, 144–47

Poehl, Karl Otto, 8, 53

Poincaré, Raymond, 110
Porter, Cole, 154

Reagan, Ronald, 27
Ricardo, David, 152, 154–55
Robbins, Lionel, 1–2, 4, 118–19, 149–52
Robinson, Joan, 150
Rutledge, John, 32, 58–59, 88, 92–93,
    107–8, 135, 141, 146

Samuelson, Paul A., 2–4, 15–16, 23–25,
    27, 29–35, 45–46, 50–51, 53–54, 59
Scitovsky, Tibor, 150
Solomon, Robert, 9–12, 15, 19, 22, 32, 34,
    55–56, 69, 73–74, 86, 90, 93–94, 97,
    103, 107, 110, 115, 121–22, 125, 137
Solow, Robert M., 15, 30, 149
Stalin, Joseph, 131

Thatcher, Margaret, 76, 104, 107, 130,
    145
Thorp, Willard L., 2
Truman, Harry S, 111

Viner, Jacob, 118, 155
Volcker, Paul A., 25, 27, 63, 108

Walesa, Lech, 129, 131
Wallich, Henry C., 154
Wanniski, Jude, 145
Willett, Thomas D., 19–20, 53–54, 69–70,
    83, 104, 110–11

Subject Index

Agricultural Adjustment Act, 119
Agricultural policy, 118
Argentina, 19, 141, 143
Articles of Confederation, 86, 88

Balboa (Panamanian currency), 138–39
Bank of Canada, 122
Bank of England, 93, 95, 100
Bank of France, 93, 110
Bank of Italy, 93
Bank of Japan, 31, 122
Belgium, 80, 112
"Big-bang" approach to monetary union,
  81
Big Brother phenomenon, 119–20
Bimetallic standard, 44
Bologna-Claremont series, 1–3, 117
Bonn Summit, 63
Brazil, 137, 141
Bretton Woods system, 7, 9, 67
Britain. See United Kingdom
Bulgaria, 124
Bundesbank, 7–8, 31, 37–40, 42–43, 47,
  50, 55, 71, 77, 82–83, 87, 92–95, 98, 102

Canada, 6, 20–21, 45, 114–16, 122–23
Canadian dollar, 122–23
Canadian Economic Policy Review
  Board, 122
Capital, real return on, 16–17
Capital flows, international, 9–10, 16, 18
Capital-gains tax, 26–27, 29–32, 34
Capital mobility, 10, 19–20
Central bank culture, 108–9
Chicago banking plan, 9
Chile, 49, 70, 118
Club Europa, 129
COMECON, 37
Common Agricultural Policy, 100, 118

Common Market. See European Commu-
  nity
"Constructivism," 88
Coordination, international, 61–74
Council of Economic and Finance Minis-
  ters, 77
Covered interest parity, 18
Crawling peg, 137–38
Credit crunch, in U.S., 20
Currency-board system, 71, 127, 139, 143
Czechoslovakia, 71, 124, 126, 128–29

Delors Report, 78
Denarius, 106
Direct investment, 18
Devaluation option in European Mone-
  tary System, 79–80
Deutsche mark (D-mark), 37–38, 41–42,
  44–45, 48, 68, 76, 79–80, 82, 84, 92–94,
  112, 118, 120, 139
Dollar depreciation, and U.S. price level,
  33
"Dollarization," in former USSR, 127
Dollar-yen exchange rate, 122

Eastern European monetary issues, 124–
  27
East Germany, 46, 54–55, 59–60, 134
Eurobonds, 18
European central bank, 77, 86–88, 91–94,
  112
European Community, 77–78, 93, 104,
  115
European currency unit (ecu), 53, 76, 78,
  81–82, 84–85, 92, 112
European Monetary System (EMS), 4, 7–
  9, 38–42, 45, 50, 57, 72, 77–78, 83–84,
  88, 97
European Monetary Union (EMU), 6, 12,
  55, 75, 77–78, 88–89, 97

European Parliament, 77, 84–85, 100, 103
European Payments Union (EPU), 106–7
Exchange rates: correlation between nominal and real, 21, 54; effectiveness of changes, 52–54; fixed-rate discipline, 88; pegged rates vs. unified currency, 52, 71; rate depreciation as nontariff barrier, 75; rate targeting, 67–68

Federalist papers, the, 86
Federal Reserve, 24–26, 28, 30–32, 34–35, 45, 64, 66–67, 71, 77, 87, 89–90, 93, 100, 103–4, 108–11, 116
Federal Reserve Bank of San Francisco, 42–43, 55
Franc, undervaluation, 110
France, 17–18, 37–38, 41–42, 44, 72–73, 79, 81, 84, 87–88, 92, 95, 107
Frankfurt, 59, 65

GATT. *See* General Agreement on Tariffs and Trade
Gdansk shipyards, 130
General Agreement on Tariffs and Trade, 73–74, 116–17
Germany: capital exporter, 7–10, 17; dominant position, 90–91; hyperinflation, 87–88, 94–95; as locomotive, 23; 1948 currency reform, 127, 132; policy mix, 27–28; price level, 47; as role model, 94–95; as source of aid to former USSR, 145; unification, 3, 37–60; wage bargaining, 112–13
Gnomes of Zurich, 25
Gold, 67–69, 94, 137
Gold standard, 94
Gosbank, 132, 144–45
Great Depression, 109–10
Greece, 78, 80
Group of Seven (G-7), 22, 61, 66–67, 69, 72, 74, 122–23
Growth recession, 24
Guilder, 42
Gulf War, 4, 78, 147

Hedging, in futures market, 97
Homo economicus, 127, 130
Hong Kong, 22, 70–71, 128–31

House of Fugger, 105
Hungary, 71, 118, 124–25, 128, 130
Hyperinflation, 87, 95, 125

Iceland, 89
Interest rates, 13–15, 29, 31, 37, 43, 61
International Monetary Fund (IMF), 7, 9, 81, 145
International monetary reform, 117
International policy coordination, 61–74
Israel, 138
Italy, 18, 44, 80–81, 95, 105

Japan, 17–18, 23, 59, 80, 117, 119–22, 145

Keynes Plan, 91–92
Krakow, 129–31, 134
Kuwait, 23, 141

Länder, East German, 39–40, 47
Latin America, 19, 141–42
Legal tender, definition, 81–82
Louvre agreements, 72–73, 120
Luxembourg, 70, 81

Maastricht agreement, 4
Mexico, 6, 19, 114, 116, 137–38
Middle East, 23, 141, 147
Monetary base, as target, 67
Money-growth rate, 61, 65
Money illusion, 52–54, 56
Mundell-Fleming model, 44
Mundell-Laffer hypothesis, 54

Napoleonic Wars, 87
National Bureau of Economic Research, 23–24, 45
Netherlands, 42, 112
New Zealand, 70
Nominal GNP target, 62–65, 67, 69–70
Nontradable goods, 47–48
Nova Huta, 130, 134

OPEC, 147
Operation Desert Storm, 4
Optimum currency area, 57, 61, 111–12

Panama, 70, 138
Panic of 1907, 89
Parallel currencies, 71, 127, 136
Perestroika, 45, 49
Phillips illusion, 39
Plaza agreements, 11, 67, 72, 120
Poland, 49–50, 60, 71, 115, 118, 124–30, 134, 136, 138–41
Political union, as prerequisite for monetary union, 77–78, 83–88
Portfolio investment, 8, 18
Portugal, 78, 80
Prague School of Economics, 128
Privatization, 129–30, 133–34
Protectionism, 73, 117
Purchasing-power securities, 29, 64–65
"Pushing on a string," 31

Quebec, 122–23

Recession, in U.S., 6, 23–24, 26, 32, 36, 45
Regionalism, 6, 114–23
Robbins Memorial Lecture, 4, 149–56
Ruble, 127–28, 132, 136
Rumania, 124

Savings-and-loan crisis, 6, 16
Scotland, 87
Scottish pound notes, 82
Seigniorage, 140, 142
Shadow Open Market Committee, 62
Silver standard, 94
"Slap-in-the-face theory" of exchange intervention, 66
Social-security tax, U.S., 34–35
Soviet Union, 3–4, 115, 124–28, 143, 145, 147
Spain, 37, 80
Stagflation, 33
Sterling, 76

Sweden, 128
Switzerland, 116, 139, 144

Textile agreement, 73
"Time-inconsistency," 76, 80
Tradable goods, 47–48, 80
Trade creation, 118
Trade destruction, 118
Trade diversion, 118
Transfer payments to eastern Germany, 37, 55
Treasury interest-rate curve, 30–31

Unemployment, 4, 95
Unified currency vs. pegged exchange rates, 52, 71
United Kingdom, 17–18, 29, 45, 57–58, 77–82, 112–13, 116, 128
United States: credit crunch, 20; effect of dollar depreciation on, 33; gold stock, 68; and Japan, 117, 119; and Louvre agreements, 120–21; monetary issues, 13–22; as monetary union, 105–6; as net debtor, 22; 1903 treaty with Panama, 138–39; as optimum currency area, 57; policy dilemmas, 23–36; real long-term interest rate, 13–15; recession, 6, 23–24, 26, 32, 36, 45; social-security tax, 34–35
Uruguay Round, 116
U.S.-Canadian agreement, 115–16, 120

Velocity, monetary, 65

Wales, 87
Wall Street, 15–16
Western European monetary union, 6, 12, 55, 75, 77–78, 88–89, 97
West Germany, 46, 54–55, 59

Yen-dollar exchange rate, 122
Yugoslavia, 68, 70–71

Zero inflation as goal, 28, 32
Zloty, 71, 125, 127, 136, 139
Zollverein, 105